Ibn Battuta

IN THIS 1375 CATALAN MAP A KING OF MALI HOLDS A HUGE ORB OF GOLD
AS A SAHARAN MERCHANT APPROACHES ON A CAMEL

STREET SIGN IN TANGIER LEADING TO WHERE IBN BATTUTA IS
TRADITIONALLY BELIEVED TO BE BURIED
(Photo by Ross E. Dunn)

Ibn Battuta
in Black Africa

by

Said Hamdun and Noël King

With a New Foreword
by Ross E. Dunn

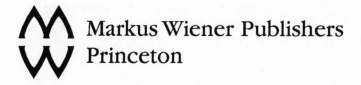 Markus Wiener Publishers
Princeton

For information write to:
Markus Wiener Publishers,
231 Nassau Street, Princeton, NJ 08542

Library of Congress Cataloging-in-Publication Data

Ibn Battuta, 1304-1377.
[Tuhfat al-nuzzâr. English. Selections]
Ibn Battuta in Black Africa/Abu Abdalla Ibn Battuta;
translated and edited with commentary by Said Hamdun and Noël King;
with a new foreword by Ross Dunn.
Originally published: London: Rex Collings, 1975. With new introduction.
Includes bibliographical references and index.
ISBN 1-55876-087-3
ISBN 1-55876-088-1 (pbk.)
1. Africa, Eastern—Description and travel—Early works to 1800.
2. Africa, West—Description and travel—Early works to 1800.
3. Ibn Battuta, 1304-1377.
I. Hamdun, Said.   II. King, Noël Quinton.   III. Title.
DT365.2.I262513   1994   94-20283
916.704—dc20   CIP

Cover Design by Cheryl Mirkin

Contents

FOREWORD
by Ross E. Dunn

TRAVELERS ARRIVING IN TOWN (BAGHDAD 635A.H./1237 A.D.)

In 1325 A.D. the young legal scholar Abu Abdallah ibn Battuta set out from his native city of Tangier on the north coast of Morocco to make the holy pilgrimage to Mecca. "I braced my resolution to quit all my dear ones," he tells us in his celebrated *Rihla,* or Book of Travels. "I set out alone, having neither fellow-traveler in whose companionship I might find cheer nor caravan whose party I might join."[1] His departure may have been poignant, but his loneliness did not last long. Within a few days he was meeting all sorts of people on the road, and as he traveled back and forth across the Eastern Hemisphere during the ensuing twenty-nine years, he made hundreds of friends, married numerous women, fathered several children, and counted among his associates eminent scholars, royal officials, rich merchants, and Mongol kings.

Indeed, one of the more fascinating aspects of Ibn Battuta's travels through the equivalent of nearly fifty modern countries is that he was repeatedly running into people he knew. Wandering lost in the remote forests of northern Turkey, he met up with "an acquaintance," who saved him and his traveling companions from perishing in a snowstorm. When he tried to make a visit *in cognito* to the Maldive Islands in the Indian Ocean, travelers who had known him in northern India 1,600 miles away recognized him and blew his cover. In southern China he met a man named al-Bushri whom he had known slightly in India and who came originally from a town in Morocco only forty miles from Tangier. About five and a half years later when he was traveling in the northern Sahara Desert at the opposite extremity of the hemisphere, he became the house guest of al-Bushri's brother! (See p. [30].)

In the age of the global village we might not be terribly surprised to bump into some old acquaintance while changing planes in Tokyo or Frankfurt. But six and a half centuries ago, when the world's population was many times less than it is now, cities were much smaller and more widely scattered, vast deserts and oceans separated settled communities, and the pace of travel was limited to the speed of horses or sailing ships, we might suppose that few people ever ventured far beyond their natal land.

In fact the caravan trails and sea lanes of the fourteenth century hummed with travelers on long-distance errands of all sorts. Among travelers, moreover, Muslims were preeminent. Because the lands of Islam dominated the center of the Eastern Hemisphere and extended nearly all the way across it, Muslim merchants moved incessantly here and there among the major regions of Eurasia and Africa carrying the greater part of the hemisphere's international trade in luxury and everyday goods. Other Muslims went abroad to make the holy pilgrimage (*hajj*) to Mecca and Medina in Arabia, a journey that might take a poor pilgrim several years. Still others traveled as diplomatic emis-

ARAB WORLD MAP BY IBN SAID, 13TH CENTURY

saries, imperial messengers, wandering mystics, or cultured scholars in search of books and famous teachers.

Islamic civilization was highly cosmopolitan in the fourteenth century in two respects. First, Islamic cities had on the whole the most heterogenous populations of residents and transient visitors of any cities in the world. This was especially true of cities of the Islamic heartland partly because the region between Egypt and Persia (what we call today the Middle East) was geographically the narrow bottleneck of the hemisphere (semi-arid steppes to the north, deserts and seas to the south) and therefore the funnel through which all the east-west trade routes passed. A diverse assortment of transients and temporary residents—Arabs, Persians, Jews, Kurds, Berbers, Turks, Greeks, Italians, and Catalans—walked the streets of Damascus, Aleppo, Jerusalem, Tabriz, Alexandria, and, most cosmopolitan of all in Ibn Battuta's time, Cairo.

Islamic internationalism was also evidenced in the collective life of the *'ulama*, the class of Muslim religious and legal scholars. In Islamic belief individuals who traveled to make the *hajj* or to further their education in the religious sciences were thought to merit divine approval. Garbed in white gown and voluminous turban, the *'alim*, or pious scholar, was a common sight on the open road as he scurried from one city to another to seek out a particular legal text, study with a celebrated teacher, or attend a religiously endowed college. Moreover, because the *'ulama* were the lettered class and the guardians and interpreters of the sacred law of Islam (*shari'a*), the more skilled and gifted among them were much in demand to fill bureaucratic posts, direct religious institutions, and lead diplomatic missions. Fourteenth century Islam was a civilization not only of many cities but many kingdoms as well. Secular sultans and princes normally regarded it as their moral duty to treat lawyers and religious doctors in their service with respect and generosity. On the other hand, rulers could be fickle about whom they favored or disfavored. Consequently, ambitious and talented scholar-bureaucrats moved frequently from capital to capital in search of prestigious and lucrative posts. And if they should for some reason irritate their princely employer, they might skip town at very short notice.

The *'ulama* of the medieval centuries might collectively be described as the best-traveled and most cosmopolitan intellectual class in world history up to that time. Their primary loyalty was not to state, nation, or tribe, but to the *dar al-Islam*, or House of Islam, the lands where Muslim populations predominated or at least where Muslim communities ruled. In Ibn Battuta's time the *dar al-Islam* extended straight across the Eastern Hemisphere. Consequently, the most mobile and best educated among the scholarly class possessed a sharper universalist vision of humankind, a broader mental grasp of the inhabited regions of Eurasia and Africa, than any other group in the world.

Lettered Muslims of North Africa or Andalusia (southern Spain) were particularly inclined to make long trips abroad, partly to fulfill the religious obligations of the *hajj*, partly to make study tours of Cairo, Damascus, and other university cities of the Middle East. From the point of view of an Egyptian or Syrian scholar, North Africa was *jazirat al-maghrib*, the "island of the west," a region of mountains and plains cut off from the center by sea and desert. Moroccan and Andalusian intellectuals were acutely conscious that they lived in the "far west." A journey to the center was an opportunity to acquire books and diplomas, commune with the best scholars, and generally immerse oneself in the cosmopolitan life. North African sojourners were likely to earn both scholarly credentials and intellectual prestige in the Middle East and so return home to honorable and well-paying jobs in service to their religious community or their king.

The career of Ibn Marzuk, a contemporary of Ibn Battuta and a scholarly luminary of the century, is a notable example of the formative influence of the Middle East on a North African *'alim*. At the age of about seven, Ibn Marzuk left his native city of Tlemcen (in western Algeria) to perform the *hajj* with his father. He remained in the Middle East throughout his childhood, studying with masters in Mecca, Medina, Jerusalem, Hebron, Alexandria, and Cairo. He returned home when he was about twenty-two to launch a brilliant career in public life. Serving at different times sultans of Granada, Tunis, and Morocco, he occupied numerous posts including envoy to the king of Castile, minister of state, and mosque preacher in three cities. He studied with more than 250 teachers and authored several works in history, ethics, and law. In his later years he returned to Cairo where he served as professor, preacher, and judge. Here was a true cosmopolite of his age.

Ibn Battuta never came close to matching Ibn Marzuk's brilliance as a scholar or public official, but he was every bit an *'alim*. He came from a respected family of jurists and judges who practiced their profession in Morocco and Andalusia. His ethnic ancestors were rural Berbers of northern Morocco, but in language and culture he was a city-dwelling Arab. In his youth he learned as much of the religious and juridical sciences— Qur'anic exegesis, the traditions of the Prophet (hadith), grammar, rhetoric, theology, logic, and law—as the mosque schools of a provincial town like Tangier could offer. More important for his traveling career, he absorbed the moral and social qualities expected of an *'alim*. These included a pious and restrained demeanor; a refined sense of discretion, protocol, personal hygiene, and proper dress; an aptitude for clever and learned conversation. From his accounts of personal experience in the *Ribla*, it is evident that even though he had no profound intellectual gifts, he was, to use the modern phrase, a "class act."

The second quarter of the fourteenth century was the twilight of the age of Mongol dominance, the extraordinary period of about a century and a half when Mongol kings, first the conqueror Chinggis Khan and then his sons and grandsons, ruled the greater part of the Eurasian land mass. At the time of Ibn Battuta's travels the unified empire of Chinggis had already broken into four Mongol successor kingdoms, all of them enormous in their own right. These four states were well-administered and reasonably stable, and their rulers continued in the best Mongol tradition to protect the long-distance trade routes and encourage merchants of all faiths and nations to use them. Moreover, even where Mongol lords did not reign, strong, commerce-minded states were the rule in the early fourteenth century. These included, among others, the Marinid kingdom of Morocco, the Mamluk Sultanate of Egypt and Syria, the Delhi Sultanate of northern India, and the Mali empire in West Africa. The existence of this chain of robust states stretching all the way across Eurasia and deep into Africa meant that inter-regional trade boomed, not only on the overland caravan trails but also on the maritime routes of the southern seas.

In other words, the second quarter of the fourteenth century

MONGOL RULER WITH AN ARAB SCRIBE (CA. 710 A.D./1310 A.D.)

was a relatively auspicious time for an adventurous Muslim to make an extended tour of the world. A traveling scholar could always hitch a ride with a caravan, and anyone who was traveling in connection with the *hajj*, whether he had any money or not, could always find rest and refreshment in a caravansary, mosque, or private home. Ironically, Ibn Battuta's career neared its end just as this relatively halcyon period was coming to a close. In 1347 the Black Death swept into the Middle East, North Africa, and Europe, heralding a half century of economic troubles, political collapse, and social upheaval that seemed to afflict nearly every part of the Eastern Hemisphere. Ibn Battuta survived the plague (though his mother did not), and he settled into the quiet, comfortable life of a judge in some provincial Moroccan town, safe from the international calamities occurring all around.

The Moroccan may have been the greatest traveler of his era, but he was not an aimless wanderer. His motives for going to particular places varied. First of all, he traveled, like tens of thousands of Muslims in the fourteenth century, to perform the rites of the *hajj* at the holy places of Mecca in western Arabia. He left home, he tells us, "swayed by an overmastering impulse within me and a desire long-cherished in my bosom to visit these illustrious sancturaries"[2]. In the course of his career he participated in the rituals of the *hajj* season six or seven times, each time presumably accruing divine merit. Indeed, Mecca became the hub of his tours. During most of his years on the road he was either traveling away from Arabia or returning to it.

Second, he traveled, as so many *'ulama* did, to pursue advanced studies in Islamic law, though in fact he never put much time into them. With the exception of a few months of study with teachers in Damascus (and possibly more time in Mecca), he never settled into the routine of listening to lectures and mastering learned texts, which was the only route to genuine intellectual proficiency.

Third, he traveled as a devotee of Sufism, which was the mystical, ecstatic dimension of Islam. Through Sufi learning and practice the individual sought personal communion with God, usually under the guidance of a saintly master. In the fourteenth century Sufi ideas and practices were becoming fully incorporated into Islamic orthodoxy, very notably in North Africa. Ibn Battuta journeyed to a number of places specifically to visit living scholar-saints who possessed an abundance of *baraka*, the quality of divine grace that might be imparted to disciples and devotees. He reports in the *Rihla* that on several occasions he was tempted to settle down to a life of Sufi spirituality, though the lure of the road invariably overpowered him.

Fourth, he traveled to seek employment and generous rewards in government service. He almost certainly lacked the scholarly credentials to secure a worthy post as a jurist in a city such as Cairo or Damascus, where brilliant lawyers abounded and the competition was stiff. However, in the further lands where Islamic civilization was newer and rougher-edged and where educated cadres were in short supply, rulers were less choosy about the intellectual "résumés" of the people they employed. Ibn Battuta also commanded a certain prestige in countries such as India simply because he was an Arab and therefore a man of "the Prophet's race." He spent about eight years (1334-1341) in the Sultanate of Delhi, an Islamic kingdom of Turkic origin that had only been founded a little more than a century before his arrival. He served first as a judge, then as an administrator of a royal mausoleum, and finally as the sultan's ambassador to the Mongol court of China, though this last commission was aborted following a shipwreck off the coast of India. Later, he served for several months as chief judge in the Maldive Islands, a tiny Islamic state in the Indian Ocean.

Ibn Battuta also traveled to some places for no concrete reason at all, only to satisfy his curiosity, have an adventure, or perhaps to satisfy a prideful goal to see more of the *dar al-Islam* than anyone else ever had. In the *Rihla* he reports that he met a learned man in western Turkey who was particularly well-traveled. He takes pains, however, to list the several countries that this man had not visited and he had. "I have outdone him," he crows, "by visiting these regions."

Ibn Battuta's two trips to Africa south of the Sahara occupied only a small part of his nearly three decade career. His sea voyage from Arabia to the coasts of East Africa and back took him only about five months (the first part of 1329 or 1331, depending how one interprets the *Rihla's* chronological clues). His journey by camel caravan from Morocco to the Mali empire in West Africa, his last recorded adventure, lasted about two years (1352-1354). Even so, his narratives of these two journeys have a historical value far out of proportion to their place in his overall itinerary. The *Rihla* represents the only eye-witness account we have of both the East African city-states and the Mali empire in the fourteenth century, or for that matter the thirteenth as well. Other Arab scholars of the period compiled and reported information on these two regions, but they relied on second-hand accounts of merchants or other travelers who never wrote their own books about what they saw. Ibn Battuta's account of the East African cities of Mogadishu, Mombasa, and Kilwa is informative on a number of historical points but also brief. His report on Mali is four times longer and much richer, including detailed descriptions of the royal government. We owe Ibn Battuta a deep debt for bearing witness to the magnitude and brilliance of this grassland empire.

About twenty-three years separated Ibn Battuta's trips to East and West Africa, and each one was linked to an entirely different circuit of travel. The commercial towns stretching along the tropical coasts of what are today Somalia, Kenya, Zanzibar, Tanzania, and Mozambique belonged to the intercommunicating world of the Indian Ocean. In Ibn Battuta's time they were thoroughly Muslim towns with close economic and cultural connections to South Arabia and the lands of the Persian Gulf. Morever, the seasonal monsoon winds, which permitted sailing ships to cross open expanses of the Indian Ocean with reasonable safety and cost efficiency, connected East Africa and its commerce not only to the Middle East but also to India and ultimately China.

In the fourteenth century there may have been about forty settlements along the coast from Mogadishu southward. Except for enslaved captives and traders coming in from the East African interior, the inhabitants of the towns were Muslims. Since the early centuries of Islam, Arab or Persian merchants and other adventurers had been visiting the coast, many remaining permanently and intermarrying with local African families. The rulers and wealthy merchants of the larger ports made a point of tracing their descent from Muslim "pioneers" who had come from the heartland of Islamic civilization. However, the towns were fundamentally African; they were not Middle Eastern settler colonies. To illustrate the point, Swahili, the most widely spoken language in East Africa today, was in the fourteenth century evolving into the principal language of trade and everyday affairs along the coast. Swahili incorporates

A DHOW UNDER SAIL OFF THE COAST OF EAST AFRICA

numerous linguistic borrowings from Arabic, notably religious or political words, but it is fundamentally a Bantu African language.

The more important coastal towns imported quantities of luxury goods such as Indian cottons, Persian glassware, and Chinese pottery that contributed to the agreeable urban lifestyle of the richer households. These families, who lived in comfortable stone homes or even ornate palaces, made their fortunes mainly by exporting African products, particularly ivory, ambergris, mangrove poles, slaves, and gold. In those times the overland trade, which ran hundreds of miles into the interior, was in the hands of corporations of non-Muslim African merchants who brought goods down to the coast for transshipment. In other words, the towns would never have thrived as they did were it not for the production and commercial enterprise of the inland populations. Even so, the inhabitants of these diminutive city-states cared most about their complex economic and cultural connections with the wider world of Islam. Travelers were incessantly sailing back and forth between the coast and the northerly ports of the Arabian Sea. Ibn Battuta would not have found his voyage more than 800 miles south of the equator a particular exotic experience.

But why did he go to East Africa? He offers no explicit motive in the *Rihla*. It is possible that when he sailed from Jidda, Mecca's port on the Red Sea, to Aden, one of the major ports of the Indian Ocean trade, he was already thinking of going to India to seek a post in the Delhi Sultanate. He arrived at Aden during a period of the annual monsoon cycle when ships would not normally have been going to India. A vessel was, however, hoisting sail for the African coast. This may have been one of those occasions when he visited a new part of the Islamic world simply because it was there.

He might well have made an extended sojourn in Mogadishu or Kilwa. The local sultans of the towns were always on the lookout for lettered Arabs from abroad who might give administrative service and lend cosmopolitan prestige to their little courts. Ibn Battuta appears to have enjoyed his voyage and was particularly impressed by the Sultan of Kilwa. "This sultan is a very humble man," the *Rihla* says. "He sits with the poor people and eats with them, and gives respect to people of religion

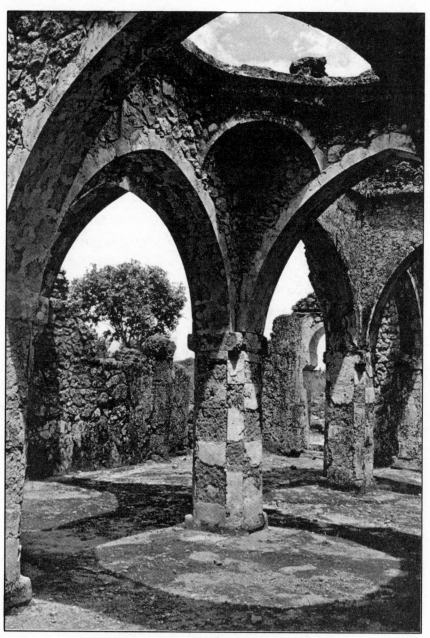

THE RUINS OF THE GREAT MOSQUE OF KILWA

and of prophetic descent." (p. [20]) Despite the warm reception he received as one of these "people of religion," he decided to return to South Arabia as soon as he could find a ship. From there he made his way back to Mecca for another *hajj* season.

He undertook his courageous journey across the Sahara to West Africa after returning home to Morocco in 1349. He may have decided to visit Mali, despite its location on the far side of the fearsome void, simply because it was one of the few Muslim kingdoms in the world he had not seen. Some scholars speculate that Abu Inan, the Sultan of Morocco and one of the more vigorous kings of the Marinid dynasty, sent Ibn Battuta to the Sudan on a diplomatic mission. The purpose of the embassy would have been to strengthen commercial ties, particularly the gold trade, between Mali and Morocco. Such a motive is plausible. The Sultan of Delhi, after all, had chosen Ibn Battuta to lead a delegation to China. Moreover, diplomatic exchanges between the kings of Mali and their North African counterparts did occasionally take place. Ibn Battuta does mention in the *Rihla* that when he was starting his homeward journey from the southern Sahara, he received a message from Abu Inan "commanding me to appear in his sublime presence." (p. [60]) On the other hand, he never states explicitly that he was traveling under orders. Since he usually reported any business he had with kings or princes in great detail, sprinkling names of the powerful and famous all over the *Rihla*, it seems likely that if Abu Inan had commissioned him to go to Mali, the traveler would have taken pains to let his readers know it. On the contrary, he berates Sulaiman, the *mansa*, or king of Mali for treating him as a person of no particular account.

Whatever Ibn Battuta's role in trans-Saharan diplomacy, there is no doubt that the Marinid government wanted Mali's trade. The auriferous mines of West Africa, which lay in savanna country near the southern frontier of the empire, supplied a large percentage of the gold that circulated in both Christian Europe and the Islamic states. Camel caravans carried it to North Africa, and from there it entered the wider Mediterranean market largely through the intermediary of Genoese, Catalan, or other European sea merchants. Indeed, the high age of the Mali kingdom from the mid thirteenth to the mid fourteenth centuries corresponded to the period when Europe was exchanging silver for gold as its principal hard currency. This prompted the European traders to offer higher and higher prices for gold in the North African ports. Europe's rising demand, coupled with the steady market in the Islamic states, spurred the mines to increase production. The *mansas* in turn profitted immensely because they took golden tribute from the local authorities who controlled the mines, and they scrupulously taxed all caravans passing through their territory.

The merchants of Mali transshipped gold northward through towns that lay along the southern edge of the desert, notably Walata, Timbuktu, Gao, and Takadda. Like the East African cities, these towns occupied a geographic frontier, in this case the transitional zone between the great desert and the quite densely populated grassland belt of West Africa that the Arab geographers called the *bilad al-sudan*, or land of black people. The northbound caravans organized in these "ports" of the Sahara

EXPORT PRODUCTS FROM MALI: IVORY AND GOLD

carried not only gold but also ivory, ostrich feathers, hides, slaves, and various other West African products. The camel trains arriving out of the desert from commercial centers at the *northern* edge of the desert, notably the Moroccan city of Sijilmasa, brought salt, textiles, horses, copper, books, paper, iron ware, spices, wheat, and a wide array of goods from the Mediterranean world.

As important as international trade was to Mali's prosperity, the economic bedrock of the empire was agriculture. Most of the subjects of the *mansas* were not town-dwellers but farmers, cattle herders, or village artisans. Mali was also an empire of considerable ethnic complexity. The core population, as well as the chiefly clan that provided the *mansas*, spoke Malinke, but peoples of diverse languages and cultural traditions paid allegiance to the imperial throne.

Mali was not the earliest large-scale West African state.

IN EXCHANGE FOR SALT

Ghana had come before it but withered away in the eleventh and twelfth centuries. The early *mansas* were regional lords of the upper valleys of the Senegal and Niger Rivers. In the thirteenth century these leaders succeeded in gaining control of territory between the gold fields of the southern savanna and the desert gateways to the north, thus positioning themselves to take tribute in gold from the populations controling the mines and to levy taxes on gold-bearing caravans. These revenues permitted the *mansas* to build up their army, which was comprised mainly of infantry bowmen and armored cavalry. As the king's forces moved east and west across the fertile savanna, more farming populations were subdued and taxed and more of the north-south flow of commerce was brought under state control. Riches flowed into the royal treasury, and the army and administration expanded even more. In the course of the thirteenth and fourteenth centuries the *mansas* extended their realm westward to the Atlantic coast, eastward past the great bend of the Niger River, and northward to the desert fringe. At some point early in the expansion of the empire the ruling family also converted to Islam. Whatever religious feeling may have motivated them, their conversion enhanced their prestige among established

A MARKET NEAR THE SITE OF OLD SIJILMASA
(Photo by Ross E. Dunn)

Muslim merchant communities of the savanna, and it opened wider possibilities for commercial and diplomatic contacts with North Africa.

Ibn Battuta had a knack for visiting Islamic kingdoms in their prime, and Mali was no exception. Just about the time he was preparing to start, Mansa Musa, the most renowned of the Mali emperors, was making his famous pilgrimage to Mecca, crossing the Sahara to Egypt with a caravan of thousands. The *mansa* and his retainers, the Arab chroniclers tell us, spread so much gold around the Cairo bazaars that for a time its price went down on the Egyptian market. Mansa Musa's undertaking of this lavish pilgrimage more than 3,500 miles from home was an indicator of the wealth, orderliness, and stability of his kingdom. Mansa Sulaiman, who came to the throne in 1341, appears to have been an equally effective ruler, though after his death in

1360 the empire gradually deteriorated.

Ibn Battuta has given us a marvelous description of Mali under Mansa Sulaiman, but he definitely had mixed feelings about the place. On the one hand he was impressed that a person could feel perfectly secure traveling hundreds of miles through the royal domains. He also regarded the Muslim population of the kingdom as pious and earnestly dedicated to their mosque prayers and Quranic studies. On the other hand, he found Sulaiman less generous toward visiting doctors of the law than he knew Mansa Musa had been. He also abhored various local practices that he thought inconsistent with Islamic rectitude and seemliness. Women went about bare-breasted, men engaged in private conversations with women who were not

CARAVAN APPROACHING TIMBUKTU
(Drawing by Heinrich Barth in 1853)

their wives, subjects of the *mansa* prostrated themselves on the ground and threw dust over their heads when they approached him. Ibn Battuta's standards were those of a cultured Arab urbanite and a righteous, if not sometimes priggish, upholder of the sacred law. He was not particularly interested in recognizing basic realities of Mali society. Most of the *mansa's* subjects were not Muslims at all but adhered to the local religions of their ancestors. Even the commercial towns were probably less thoroughly Islamicized than the East African city-states. The *mansas* incorporated Islamic rituals into their royal proceedings, they used Arabic to some extent as a language of administration, and they retained the services of numerous Muslim scribes, treasurers, and jurists, some of whom were migrants from North Africa. A few of the kings went to Mecca. On the other hand, royal legitimacy depended on the loyalty of the Malinke core population, which was largely non-Muslim and would have disapproved of any radical break with traditional cultural conventions or expectations of how kings should behave. Because Islam had reached West Africa mainly from Morocco, Ibn Battuta was perhaps unprepared for these startling cultural differences between his homeland and the *bilad al-Sudan*.

In one sense Mali and the East African coast were part of two entirely different international worlds. Mali belonged to the commercial realm of the Sahara basin and the Mediterranean. East Africa looked toward the Middle East and across the sea to India. In other ways, however, both regions were very much part of the same world, the world of expanding Islam, the world

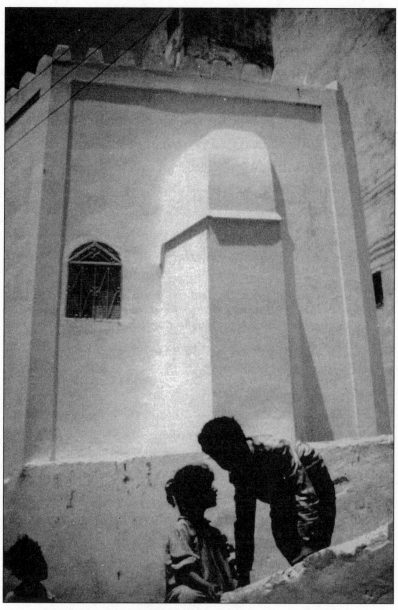

TOMB IN TANGIER WHERE IBN BATTUTA IS TRADITIONALLY
BELIEVED TO BE BURIED
(Photo by Ross E. Dunn)

of interlinked trans-hemispheric trade, the world of cosmopolitan travelers who paid little attention to political or ethnic dividing lines.

Said Hamdun and Noël King's sprightly, informal, eminently readable translation of the *Rihla's* Arabic text seems to capture Ibn Battuta, the inquisitive, urbane cosmopolite. In these pages we discover no medieval pedant or gloomy cleric but a raconteur, a charmer, and a lover of life.

Notes

1. H.A.R. Gibb, trans. and ed., *The Travels of Ibn Battuta A.D. 1325-1354, Translated with Revisions and Notes from the Arabic Text Edited by C. Defremery and B.R. Sanguinetti* (Cambridge: Cambridge University Press for the Hakluyt Society, 1958), p. 8.

2. Gibb, *Travels*, p. 8.77

INTRODUCTION
by Said Hamdun
and Noël King

LECTURE BY A FAMOUS TEACHER (IRANIAN, 16TH CENTURY)

Ibn Baṭṭūṭa, who was born at Tangier in North Africa in 1304 and died not far from there some sixty-five years later, was the greatest of the pre-modern travellers and will go down in history as being notable among the travellers of all time. Benjamin of Tudela, a Jew from Spain who in the second half of the twelfth century travelled to Baghdad and back, hardly touched central or south Asia and did not penetrate Africa. Marco Polo (1254-1324), a Christian, reached China and returned to Venice by way of south-east Asia and India, but he did not get into Africa. Chinese travellers reached Europe but did not go inland in Arabia or to West Africa, or even pass through the hinterland of Arab Africa.

On his side, ibn Baṭṭūṭa set out from his home town in North Africa at the age of twenty-one, and travelled till he was nearly fifty. He went across the countries we would today call Morocco, Algeria, Tunisia, Egypt, Israel, Lebanon and Syria, then southwards through Jordan into Arabia to Mecca. There he spent some years and from there visited Iraq and Iran as well as southern Arabia. He visited the coast of the Sudan, went back to south Arabia and from Aden went on southwards to Somalia and Tanzania. He then visited the Persian Gulf and returned to Mecca by an overland route. From there he journeyed through Egypt, Syria, Asia Minor, the Crimea and the Balkans to Constantinople; thence through southern Russia

1

and central Asia to Afghanistan, Pakistan and India. From Delhi he went to south India and the Maldives, Ceylon, Assam and Bengal (areas now in India and Bangladesh). He journeyed on through Malaysia and Indonesia to China. On returning home to Tangier he visited Spain, and finally walked across the Sahara to ancient Malli. It is the black African section of his travels which confirms his pre-eminence, and it is this part of his narrative which is the subject of this book.

Besides the places he visited and the incredible distances he travelled on foot or on the backs of horses and camels, ibn Baṭṭūṭa is notable for the picture he gives of the Islamic world of his day. This came nearest to being the first genuinely world civilization which ever existed before the Americas and Australia were added to 'the known world'. Ibn Baṭṭūṭa as a person from a North African town could feel genuinely part of it. By descent he was Berber—and nobody knows how long ago the Berbers came to Africa—history mentions them hundreds of years before it tells of people speaking Bantu languages; they are about as African as anybody can be. By language and culture he was an Arab and a Muslim. This sharing in the world of Islam meant he could travel without money or resources and everywhere find he could understand and be understood, obtain hospitality as well as rich gifts from rulers or from Muslim merchants. It is true that in some respects Islamic civilization had passed its zenith: the Arab conquests of the first Islamic century since the migration of the Prophet to Medina in A.D. 622 had been followed up by the rise of the superb civilizations of the Maghrib (north-western Africa), Egypt, Syria, Iraq and Persia. The Empire of the Caliphs and other parts of the Islamic

2

world had suffered much at the hands of the Mongols who took Baghdad in 1258, and, in ibn Baṭṭūṭa's own day, the Black Death was to decimate whole countrysides. But following the Mongol opening up of Central Asia, Islamic civilization was able to penetrate even more widely. The new peoples coming westwards from Central Asia of 'Turkish' background were converted, and glorious Muslim civilizations arose in Turkey and India.

In the meantime, Islam had journeyed far into Africa and South-East Asia and there were flourishing Muslim communities and outposts in West and East Africa as well as in Malaysia and Indonesia. Ibn Baṭṭūṭa sets before us a breathtaking panorama of a civilization which included or touched upon every part of the world other than the Americas and Australia. He gives us an unforgettable picture of Islamic culture, hospitality, scholarship and holiness.

As a bonus, from his own description, we learn a great deal about the man himself, in fact, there are few pre-modern people of whom we can obtain so vivid a picture. We get to know a very remarkable human being, who is somehow so real and like ourselves that soon we enter the more deeply into the narrative and see things through his eyes. He is insatiably curious and his interests are impressively wide. He is concerned not only with kings, politics, geography, routes and wealth; but also he takes an intense interest in local products, especially the food and the women. He has deep prejudices, for instance, against schismatics in Islam whose views differ from his own, and against unbelievers and rationalists. Yet reading these travels is a sure antidote to the eurocentricity of most American and European

3

medieval historians, for here we have a writer who could view things Magribian, Egyptian, Syrian, Byzantine, Persian, Arabian, Indian, Chinese, Italian, Spanish and African with the same impartial acceptances, enjoyments and rejections.

Ibn Baṭṭūṭa has his pettinesses. He loves name-dropping: trying to impress us by reciting the names of the people whom he met or with whom he was connected in scholarly learning or holiness. Yet it was these connections which were his 'traveller's cheques' which produced funds from donors as he travelled. He loves a fine spectacle, and his pages are full of the pomp and circumstance of parades and processions. Yet his book was intended to entertain as well as instruct and, despite oneself, using ibn Baṭṭūṭa as proxy, one enjoys the triumph, the glory and the splendour of it all. This world-traveller is something of an old prude; he gets quite upset at seeing young women whose breasts had formed going round in the nude, but he is equally outraged in a men's public bath to find men bathing without loincloths.

He enjoys his dignity and comforts. He lets slip that he never travels without a slave-girl or two, and he is avaricious in his desire for rich donations from Muslim rulers and not averse to drawing their attention to their duty to give him gifts by means which fall little short of blackmail. He carefully puts down anyone who might claim to have travelled as much as he has. He does not fail to report his illnesses. He seems to have experienced most travellers' diseases from Lahore sore to Delhi belly. Only the fact that the New World had not been discovered saved him from Montezuma's revenge.

Yet ibn Baṭṭūṭa is a man of courage. He never reveals any fear of the ocean, though he did not take to sea travel till comparatively late in his career and faced some terrifying storms. He loves luxury and yet he received his calling to be a traveller almost as Saint Paul received his vocation to Apostleship. Ibn Baṭṭūṭa betrays that he would have enjoyed a regular home life and seeing his children grow up before his eyes. He was also generous to others and sensitive to their suffering, whether they were Hindu women committing *sutee* or slave-boys thirsty in the desert. For a man who is so interesting a character and who achieved so much, it is surprising how little about him his contemporaries have passed on to us.

Ibn Ḥajar of Ascalon who died in A.D. 1448 has a note about ibn Baṭṭūṭa in his *Hidden Pearls*.[1] He gives his name in full as 'Muḥammad ibn Abdallāh ibn Muḥammad ibn Ibrāhīm ibn Muḥammad ibn Ibrāhīm ibn Yūsuf of the Luwāta tribe [a Berber group] and the city of Tangier'. He says that ibn Khaṭīb remarks (to translate colloquially): 'He had not too much of what it takes.' Gibb translates this as: 'He had a modest share of the sciences.'[2] Presumably the meaning is that he was not really a scholar. The biographer gives ibn Khaṭīb's summary of ibn Baṭṭūṭa's travels and goes on to say that ibn Marzūq reported that ʿAbdallāh ibn Juzayy was told to write up the traveller's narrative by the sultan; ibn Baṭṭūṭa was suspected of telling lies but ibn Marzūq considered him innocent.[3] He also reports that he lived on till the seventieth year of the eighth Muslim century (A.D. 1368-1369), and died while serving as *qāḍi* in some town or another. He remarks on his pre-eminence as a traveller and adds that he was a very generous and gracious person.

The only other contemporary material we have is to be found in ibn Khaldūn's *Muqaddimah*.[4] He says that when ibn Baṭṭūṭa, a shaikh from Tangier, returned to the Maghrib after twenty years of travel, he told many stories, especially about India. It was suspected that he was a liar, but ibn Khaldūn consulted one of the court officials who told him of a man who was put in prison with his son and the boy grew up therein. The lad asked his father about the animals whose flesh was served to them—mutton, beef, camel-meat. However well his father described them, for the boy sheep, cows and camels were only types of rat, for rats were the only animals he had seen.

Bearing this salutary parable in mind, we too must ask to what extent we can trust this narrative. It is clear that now and then ibn Baṭṭūṭa succumbs to every traveller's or raconteur's temptation to embellish his narrative. Thus, when he had reached the Black Sea, he gives a rather suspicious narrative of a visit to Bulghar in which he covered about a thousand miles in less than two weeks. When travelling in far eastern seas on the way to China he tells of a visit to a state which is ruled by women; historians find great difficulty in locating it. On the way back from China he tells of a storm after which they saw a shape like a mountain and his companions said it was the *ruq*, an enormous bird which would destroy them if it saw them. Luckily the wind changed and they got away. Even so, he does not actually say he saw it. These are the most notable examples in the whole narrative, and even with them it is cruel to compare him with Gulliver, though the *ruq* may just remind us of Sindbad.

In the main, ibn Baṭṭūṭa himself is one of the most reliable sources that has come down to us from pre-modern times. To say this is not to guarantee everything in the *Travels*. A traveller

6

IBN BATTUTA IN BLACK AFRICA

JOURNEYS 1326, 1329–30, 1352–53

- - - - - - Main routes
········· Place names mentioned in text

Sijilmāsa   Place names mentioned in text
BARDĀMA   Area & Tribal names mentioned in text
Nairobi   Modern & other places not mentioned in these journeys
Senegal   Names of natural features
AIR   Saharan massifs (generalized)

of this kind could hardly carry elaborate notes or send home regular reports. Moreover, ibn Baṭṭūṭa underwent such adventures as shipwreck and an armed robbery which left him with only his trousers. The man obviously had a prodigious memory —but the best of memories can deceive, especially where the same place is visited more than once. The old gentleman's narrative was dictated to a scribe who would inevitably make a few mistakes. It was edited by ibn Juzayy, who in his description of his task states that the sultan told ibn Baṭṭūṭa to dictate a description of the places he had seen, of the happenings he remembered, and of the kings, scholars and holy men he had met. The resultant narrative was interesting in itself, gave joy to the reader and hearer as well as being instructive. Ibn Juzayy's task was to put it together in the form of a work which brought out the usefulness of the material, caused it to conform to elegant literary usage, and made it generally suitable for pleasure in reading and edification. Sometimes he had re-expressed ibn Baṭṭūṭa's meaning in his own words but often he had used the traveller's own narrative. He had not attempted to verify anything, for ibn Baṭṭūṭa himself vouches for what he has seen and clearly states what is hearsay. He (ibn Juzayy) had indicated the full pronunciation of strange names and sounds by indicating vowels where necessary.[5]

After ibn Juzayy and the first scribe had finished, the manuscript had to be copied. Luckily there are available at the *Bibliotheque Nationale* in Paris some excellent manuscripts. Indeed, part of one of them may have come from the hands of ibn Juzayy himself. Defrémery and Sanguinetti, the French editors on whose printed text this translation is based, used good manuscripts, but here and there we have had to reject their readings or emendations. We also consulted the Beirut edition but a thoroughly critical text with a full apparatus of variants has still to be produced.

Ibn Juzayy ends his work of editing with the remark: 'It would not be concealed from anybody of sound mind that this shaikh [ibn Baṭṭūṭa] was the traveller of the age, and he who says this man is the [supreme] traveller of this community [Islam] would not be far from the truth'. This tribute remains true six centuries later, and indeed one could say even more in praise of this great man. It is hoped that this work will do a little to make him better known in his own continent which may produce the greatest travellers of coming ages.

It remains to describe briefly how our work came to be written and to give thanks to the many who have helped us. This book originated at Makerere University College at Kampala, Uganda, in 1965. Said Hamdun wanted an Arabic narrative to read with Noel King, for the latter had worked at grammars, handbooks and holy books for years and needed something more flowing and less deadly serious. We settled on ibn Baṭṭūṭa's travels in black Africa, partly because its Arabic is so beautiful, because his narrative is by an African in the big sense of that word and tells us so much about Islam in Africa, and, besides, he was a scholar of Religious Studies. As we went forward it began to seem to Noel King a shame that the running verbal translation by Said Hamdun, himself an African and a Muslim who had studied also in Europe and America, should not reach a wider audience. The text we used for translation was the Arabic of Defrémery and Sanguinetti: *Voyages d'Ibn*

9

Batoutah, four volumes, Paris, third edition, 1893-1895.[6] The relevant volume number of this work is given in large Roman numerals at the beginning of a passage and the page references are given as they occur within brackets. Noel King copied the consonantal text, Said Hamdun then pointed it and translated it orally. The former transcribed and added notes, many of which were also based on the latter's oral remarks. The work was finished in 1968, but was then overtaken by the misfortunes which collaborative work undergoes when both members are transferred—the one to California in 1968 and the other to Kenya in 1970. In 1973 we returned to the typescript and felt the translation would suffer by total revision, even if we had the time. A great deal has happened in scholarship concerning Africa, especially in Manding studies in these last four years. We cannot claim to be abreast of the experts but we hope the notes, which have been extensively revised, give a true indication of where the action is for those who wish to go into academic detail.

Our debt to the scholars whose writings made our journey so much easier than their own pioneer efforts, ranging from the editors of the text to Sir Hamilton Gibb, is inadequately acknowledged by mentioning their books and articles in the annotated Bibliography. We also thank other scholars for reading through our efforts and making many suggestions and corrections. Dr Humphrey Fisher of the School of Oriental and African Studies at London consistently helped our work in Africa over a period of years: checking out references, revising translations, obtaining photocopies and corresponding faithfully. He and Professor John O. Hunwick looked through the translation and made many helpful suggestions. The Manding and other specialist material was also provided by the latter. Professor W. Montgomery Watt has also given a great deal of help and encouragement. Dr Pierre Cachia, Dr Richard Randolph and Dr Edmund Burke have kindly verified references for us. More recently, Dr Aziz Batran, himself a Sudanese, has gone over our work in detail and assisted in making the notes more up-to-date. For the map we are indebted to Dr David McMaster of the Centre of African Studies and Mr Carson Clarke of the Department of Geography of the University of Edinburgh. Mrs Joan Hodgson of the Inter-Library Loan Desk at the Library at University of California, Santa Cruz, obtained copies of books and manuscripts for us from near and far, giving us such superb service that we did not regret not being able to go in person to Dakar, London, Montreal, Washington, Berkeley and the other places whence she culled our material. The proofs were corrected at Port Moresby and such reference checking as was possible was thanks to the assistance of the Reader Services Staff of the University Library there. We also gratefully thank those who have laboured with the sub-editing, checking of references and typing—Evelyn, Francis and Jeremy King, Alan and Clare Claydon, Mrs Anne Kawuki, Mrs Dot Bergen, Amanda Tanwell and Miss Lilia Osuna.

Mawlid al-Nabī (S.A.W.),
12 Rabī al-awal 1393 A.H.   SAID HAMDUN
Palm Sunday, 15 April 1973 A.D.   and NOEL KING
Nairobi, Kenya and
Santa Cruz, California

11

NOTES TO INTRODUCTION

[1] *Al-Durar al-Kāmina*, Hyderabad, Andra Pradesh, III, 1929, pp. 480-481.

[2] Ibn Khatīb was an official of the court at Grenada who died in 1374. The quotation of H. A. R. Gibb is from his Hakluyt edition and translation of *The Travels of Ibn Baṭṭūṭa*. Cambridge, 1958, vol I, p. ix. We shall herafter abbreviate references to this series as 'Gibb: Hakluyt' and give the page and volume number. The Introduction to the whole work is in volume I and the East African section in volume II. The West African section is in volume IV which has not yet been published. Our debt to Gibb is great and we follow his chronology of his Hakluyt series where available, otherwise that of his *Selections* (London, 1929). Sometimes we have accepted the chronological revisions of Ivan Hrbek, 'The Chronology of Ibn Baṭṭūṭa's Travels', *Archiv Orientální*, XXX, 1962, pp. 409-486.

[3] Ibn Marzūq came from Tlemsen in Algeria, held an important post for some years in Cairo and died in 1379. Ibn Juzayy was a scholar who came from Grenada and died in 1356 or 1358. He was clearly an editor and writer of some brilliance and we owe him much, especially for his forbearance with some of the apparently whimsical but inimitable details the traveller gives. The sultan of Morocco was Abū ʿInān who reigned 1348-1358.

[4] *An Introduction to History*, translated by Franz Rosenthal, Princeton, vol. I, 1958, pp. 369-371.

[5] C. Defrémery et B. R. Sanguinetti, *Voyages d'Ibn Batoutah*, Paris, 1893, vol. I, pp. 9-12; Gibb: Hakluyt, vol. I, pp. 5-7.

[6] The edition of 1854 has been recently reprinted with preface and notes by Vincent Monteil, Paris (the Preface is dated 1968).

THE EAST AFRICAN
JOURNEY

ʿAdan, Zailaʿ, Maqdashaw. (Middle or late January, A.D. 1331)
[Ibn Baṭṭūṭa had travelled from his home in Tangier to perform the Pilgrimage. After doing so he stayed at Mecca for two years, then he travelled to Jeddah, was driven by a storm to Ra's al-Dawā'ir and Suakin on the African side of the Red Sea, returned to Arabia, visited Yemen and found his way to ʿAdan [Aden]. There he was able to take a ship sailing to East Africa on the northeast monsoon]
[I 1] In the name of God the merciful, the compassionate . . .
[II 179] I travelled from the town of ʿAdan [Aden] by sea for four days and arrived [180] at the city of Zailaʿ [Zeila], the city of the Barbara, who are a people of the blacks; Shāfiʿī by rite.[1] Their country is a desert which extends for a two months' journey, its beginning is at Zailaʿ and its ending is at Maqdashaw [Mogadishu]. Their livestock are camels and their sheep are famed for their fatness. The inhabitants of Zailaʿ are black in colour and the majority are Rejecters [*Rāfiḍi*].[2] It is a big city and has a great market but it is the dirtiest, most desolate and smelliest town in the world. The reason for its stink is the quantity of fish and the blood of the camels they butcher in its alleyways. When we arrived there we preferred to pass the night on the sea, though it was rough. We did not spend the night in the town because of its squalor.

Then we travelled thence by sea for fifteen nights and arrived at Maqdashaw [Mogadishu]. It is a town endless in its size. Its people have many camels [181], of which they slaughter hundreds every day and they have many sheep. Its people are powerful merchants. In it are manufactured the cloths named after it which have no rival, and are transported as far as Egypt and elsewhere.

One of the customs of the people of this city is that when a ship arrives at the anchorage, the *ṣunbūqs* (these are small boats) come out to it. In every *ṣunbūq* is a group of young people of the town, and every one of them brings a covered dish with food in it. He offers it to one of the merchants of the ship and says, 'This is my guest.' Each one of them does similarly. When the merchant disembarks from the ship he goes nowhere but to the house of his host from among these young people. But a man who has frequented the place a good deal and obtained a knowledge of its people may lodge where he wishes. When he lodges with his host, he [the host] sells his goods for him [182] and buys on his behalf. He who buys from him at too low a price or sells to him without the presence of his host—that transaction is considered as rejected.[3] There is profit for them in this custom.

When the young people came to the ship on which I was, one of them came to me. My companions told him, 'This is not a merchant but a *faqīh*'.[4] He shouted to his companions and said to them, 'This is the guest of the *qāḍī*.' One of the *qāḍī*'s people was among them and he informed him of that. The *qāḍī* came to the shore of the sea with a group of students and sent one of them to me. I disembarked with my travelling companions and saluted the *qāḍī* and his company. He said to me, 'In the name of God, let us go to greet the shaikh.' And I said: 'Who is the

16

shaikh?' He said, 'The sultan.' And it is their custom to speak of the sultan as the shaikh. I said to him, 'When I have lodged I will go to him.' He said to me 'It is the custom when a *faqīh* [183] or a *sharīf* or a man of piety comes, that he does not lodge till he has seen the sultan.'[5] I went with them to him as they requested.

AN ACCOUNT OF THE SULTAN OF MAQDASHAW

The sultan of Maqdashaw, as we mentioned, they only call 'the shaikh'. And his name is Abū Bakr son of shaikh 'Umar. He is in origin from the Barbara, and his speech is Maqdishī, but he knows the Arabic tongue. It is customary when a ship arrives for the sultan's *sunbūq* to go out to it. Questions are then asked about the ship, whence it comes, who is its owner, who its *rubbān* (that is, the captain), what its cargo and who of merchants and others has come on it. All that is ascertained and made known to the sultan. Then he gives lodging to him who deserves it near his house. When I arrived with the *qāḍī* whom I mentioned—and he is known as ibn al-Burhān, an Egyptian [184] by origin[6]—at the house of the sultan, one of the young men came out and greeted the *qāḍī* who said to him, 'Take this message with which you are entrusted and let *mawlānā*[7] [our master] the shaikh know that this man has come from the land of al-Ḥijāz [in Arabia].' He did so, then returned bringing with him a dish with some betel leaves and areca nuts on it.[8] He gave me ten leaves and a small quantity of nuts. He gave similarly to the *qāḍī* and what remained on the dish to my travelling companions and the students of the *qāḍī*. And he brought a sprinkler

17

of Damascene rose water which he sprinkled over me and the *qāḍī*.[9] And he said, '*Mawlānā* commands that he lodge in the Scholars' House.' (This is the house prepared for students of Religious Studies.) The *qāḍī* took my hand and we came to that house which is near the shaikh's house. And it was bedded out and set up with what is necessary. Then he came with food from the shaikh's house. With him was one of his *wazīrs* who was in charge of guests.[10] He said, '*Mawlānā* gives you *al-salāmu ʿalaikum* and he says to you, you are most welcome.' Then he put down [185] the food and we ate. Their food is rice cooked with ghee placed on a large wooden dish.[11] They put on top dishes of *kūshān*—this is the relish, of chicken and meat and fish and vegetables. They cook banana before it is ripe in fresh milk and they put it on a dish, and they put sour milk in a dish with pickled lemon on it and bunches of pickled chillies, vinegared and salted, and green ginger and mangoes.[12] These are like apples but they have a stone, and when they ripen they are very sweet and are eaten like fruit. But before they ripen they are bitter like lemons and they pickle them in vinegar. When they eat a ball of rice, they eat after it something from these salted and vinegared foods. Now one of the people of Maqdashaw habitually eats as much as a group of us would. [186] They are extremely large and fat of body. Then when we had eaten, the *qāḍī* left us.

We stayed three days and food was brought to us thrice a day, for that is their custom. When it was the fourth day, a Friday, the *qāḍī* and the students and one of the *wazīrs* of the shaikh came to me. They brought me a suit of their clothing—a silk wrapper to tie around the middle instead of trousers (which

18

they do not know), an upper garment of Egyptian linen with markings, a lined gown of Jerusalem material, and an Egyptian turban with embroideries. They also brought garments for my companions befitting their circumstances. We went to the grand mosque and prayed behind the *maqṣūra*.[13] When the shaikh came out of the gate of the *maqṣūra*, I greeted him together with the *qāḍī*. He welcomed me and spoke in their language to the *qāḍī*. Then he said in the Arabic language, 'You are most welcome. [187] You have honoured our country and given us pleasure.'

He came out to the courtyard of the mosque. He stopped at the grave of his father who was buried there. He read [from the Qur'ān] and prayed. Then the *wazirs*, the *amīrs*, and the commanders of the soldiers came and greeted him. Their custom in greeting is like the custom of the people of the Yaman. A man puts his index finger on the ground, then raises it to his head, saying: 'May God prolong your might.' Then the shaikh came out of the gate of the mosque, put on his sandals and ordered the *qāḍī* to put on his sandals and me to do the same. He turned to walk towards his house which is near the mosque. All of the people walked barefoot, and there were raised over his head four canopies of coloured silk and on the top of each canopy was the figure of a bird in gold. His clothes that day were a robe of green Jerusalem stuff and underneath it fine loose robes of Eygpt.[14] He was dressed with a wrapper [188] of silk and turbanned with a large turban. Before him drums and trumpets and pipes were played, the *amīrs* of the soldiers were before and behind him, and the *qāḍī*, the *faqīhs*, the *sharīfs* were with him. He entered his council room; in that order, the

19

wazirs, *amirs* and the commanders of the soldiers sat down there in the audience chamber. A mat was spread out for the *qāḍī* on which nobody may sit with him; the *faqīhs* and *sharīfs* were by him. They continued in this manner till the afternoon prayer, and when they had prayed the *ʿasr* [the late afternoon prayer] with the shaikh, all the soldiers came and stood in lines in accordance with their ranks. Then the drums, pipes, trumpets and the flutes were played. When these are sounded no one moves nor does he shift his position; he who is walking stops and does not move either forward or backward. When they finish beating the drums they greet with their fingers as we have described [189] and go out. That is a custom of theirs every Friday.

When it is Saturday the people come to the door of the shaikh and they sit in covered halls outside the house. The *qāḍī*, the *faqīhs*, the *sharīfs*, the men of piety, the shaikhs and the men who have performed the pilgrimage enter the second council room. They sit on wooden platforms prepared for the purpose. The *qāḍī* is on a platform by himself and each group on a platform reserved for them which nobody shares with them. Then the shaikh sits in his council and sends for the *qāḍī* who sits on his left. Then enter the *faqīhs* and their leaders sit in front of him while the rest of them salute and go away. Then the *sharīfs* enter, their leaders sit before him, the rest of them salute and go away. If they are guests, they sit on his right. Then enter the shaikhs and those who have performed the pilgrimage, and their great ones sit and the rest salute and go away. Then enter [190] the *wazirs* and *amirs*; the heads of the soldiers, rank upon rank, they salute and go. Food is brought and the *qāḍī*, the *sharīfs* and

20

whoever is sitting in that session eat with the shaikh and the shaikh eats with them. If he wishes to honour one of the leaders of his *amīrs*, he sends for him that he should eat with them. The rest of the people eat in the dining hall and their eating is according to precedence in the manner of their entrance before the shaikh. Then the shaikh goes into his house and the *qāḍī*, the *wazīrs*, the private secretary, and four of the leading *amīrs* sit for hearing litigation between the members of the public and hearing the cases of people with complaints. In a matter connected with the rules of the *sharīʿa* [religious law] the *qāḍī* passes judgement; in a matter other than that, the members of the council pass judgement, that is, the ministers and the *amīrs*.[15] In a matter where there is need of consultation with the sultan, they write about it to him and he sends out the reply to them immediately on the back of the note [191] in accordance with his view. And such is always their custom.

Then I sailed from the city of Maqdashaw going towards the land of the *Sawāḥil* [coasts], intending to go to the city of Kulwā [Kilwa] which is one of the cities of the land of the Zunūj.[16]

We arrived at the island of Manbasā (and the manner of writing its name is: the 'm' has an 'a', the 'n' is without a vowel, the 'b' has one dot and a short vowel 'a', the 's' is without dots and with a short vowel 'a' and a 'y' [which acts as a terminal 'a']).[17] Manbasā [Mombasa] is a large island with two days' journey by sea between it and the land of the *Sawāḥil*. It has no mainland. Its trees are the banana, the lemon, and the citron. They have fruit which they call the *jammūn*, which is similar to the olive and its stone is like its stone except that it is extremely sweet.[18] There

21

is no cultivation of grain among the people of this island: food is brought to them from the *Sawāhil*. The greater part of their food is bananas and fish. They are Shāfi'ī by rite, they are a religious people, trustworthy and righteous. Their mosques are made of wood, expertly built. At every door [192] of the mosques there are one or two wells. The depth of their wells is a cubit or two. They take water from them in a wooden container into which a thin stick of a cubit's length has been fixed. The ground around the well and the mosque is level. He who wants to enter the mosque washes his feet and enters. There is at its gate a piece of thick matting upon which he rubs his two feet. He who wants to make the ablution holds the pot between his thighs and pours water upon his hands and carries out the ablutions. All the people walk barefoot. We spent the night on this island and travelled by sea to the city of Kulwā [Kilwa].¹⁹ [Kulwa is] a great coastal city. Most of its people are Zunūj, extremely black. They have cuttings on their faces like those on the faces of the Līmiyyīn of Janāda.²⁰ One of the merchants told me that the city of Sufāla [Sofala] is half a month's journey from the city of Kulwā and that between [193] Sufāla and Yūfī in the land of the Līmiyyīn is a month's journey and from Yūfī gold dust is brought to Sufāla. The city of Kulwā is amongst the most beautiful of cities and most elegantly built. All of it is of wood, and the ceiling of its houses are of *al-dīs* [reeds]. The rains there are great. They are a people devoted to the Holy War because they are on one continuous mainland with unbelieving Zunūj. Their uppermost virtue is religion and righteousness and they are Shāfi'ī in rite.

22

RUINS OF KILWA

Its sultan at the time of my entry into Kulwā was Abū al-Muẓaffar Ḥasan whose *kunya* was Abū al-Mawāhib [father of gifts] because of his many gifts and deeds of generosity.[21] He was much given to razzias upon the land of the Zunūj; he raided them and captured booty. He used to set aside one fifth of it, which he spent in the ways indicated in the book of God the Exalted. He put the share of the kindred [of the prophet, the *sharīfs*] in a treasury by itself. When the *sharīfs* came to him [194] he gave it to them. The *sharīfs* used to come to him from ʿIrāq and Ḥijāz and other places. I saw at his place a group of the *sharīfs* of Ḥijāz, amongst them Muḥammad bin Jammāz, Manṣūr bin Lubaida bin Abū Numayy and Muḥammad bin Shumaila bin Abū Numayy, and I met at Maqdāshaw Tabl bin Kubaish bin Jammāz who was intending to come to him. This sultan is a very humble man. He sits with the poor people [*faqīrs*] and eats with them, and gives respect to people of religion and of prophetic descent.

A STORY CONCERNING THE SULTAN OF KULWĀ'S DEEDS OF GENEROSITY

I was present with him on a Friday when he came out from the prayer and was returning to his house. He was confronted on the road by one of the Yemeni *faqīrs*. He said to him, 'O father of gifts.' He replied, 'At your service, O *faqīr*, what is your need?' He said, 'Give me these clothes which you are wearing.' He replied, 'Yes, I will give them to you.' He said to him, 'This very moment.' He said, 'Yes, this very moment.' He went back to the mosque and went into the house of the preacher [_k̲ẖatīb_]. He put on other clothes and took off those [195] clothes. He said to the _faqīr_, 'Enter and take them.' So the _faqīr_ went in, tied them in a piece of cloth and put them on his head and went away. The gratitude of the people to the sultan increased at the evidence of his humility and graciousness. His son and heir-apparent took that suit of clothes from the _faqīr_ and compensated him for it with ten slaves. When the news reached the sultan of the gratitude of the people to him for that deed he ordered the _faqīr_ to be given in addition ten head of fine slaves and two loads of ivory. (The greater part of their gifts are ivory and seldom do they give gold.) When this honourable and generous sultan was gathered to God (may God have mercy on him), his brother Dā'ūd succeeded him. He was the opposite from him. When a beggar came to him he said to him, 'He who used to give has died, and he did not leave anything after him to be given.' The visitors would stay at his house many months and then he would give them a little, until visitors stopped coming to his door. We went by sea from Kulwā to the city of Ẓafār al Ḥumūḍ which is at the end of the land of the Yaman [in Arabia].[22]

THE WEST AFRICAN JOURNEY

TIMBUKTU
(Drawing by René Caillé in 1878)

IBN BAṬṬŪṬA'S LAST JOURNEY—MOROCCO
ACROSS THE SAHARA TO WEST AFRICA AND BACK[23]
(753 A.H., 1352 A.D. TO 754/1353)

[Ibn Baṭṭūṭa's visit to East Africa was carried out when he was still a young man. After many adventures in central Asia, India, the Maldive Islands and as far afield as China, he returned home to Tangier. Even so he could not sit still and went to visit Spain. Then he returned home but could not resist the lure of the most terrible journey of all—across the desert to the land of the blacks.]

[IV 376] A RESUMPTION . . .

I travelled from Marrākush in the company of the exalted caravan of our Lord [the sultan of Morocco] (may God support him) and we arrived at the city of Salā, then at the city of Miknāsa, the wonderful, the green, the many-flowered, which has gardens and orchards surrounding it and is in a sea of plantations of olive trees in all directions. Then we arrived at the capital Fās [Fez] (may God Most High protect her!) There I took leave from our Lord (may God give him support!) and I left in my travelling clothes for the land of the blacks [bilād as-Sūdān]. I arrived at the town of Sijilmāsa. It is a lovely city. In it there are a great deal of sweet dates. The town of Baṣra is like it for the abundance of its dates, but the dates of Sijilmāsa are sweeter.

29

The kind of date called *irār* has no like anywhere. I stayed there with the *faqīh* Abū Muḥammad al Bushrī [377]—he whose brother I met in the town of Qanjanfū [Kuang-chou near Canton?] in the land of China. How far apart they are! He was generous to the extreme. And I bought camels there and their fodder for four months.

Then I travelled at the beginning of the month of God, Muḥarram, in the year 'fifty-three [753 A.H., 18 February A.D. 1352] with travel companions whose leader was Abū Muhammad Yandakān al-Massūfī, may God have mercy on him. In the company was a group of the merchants of Sijilmāsa and others. We arrived after twenty-five days at Taghāzā. It is a village with no good in it. Amongst its curiosities is the fact that the construction of its houses and its mosques is of rock salt with camel skin roofing and there are no trees in it, the soil is just sand. In it is a salt mine. It is dug out of the ground and is found there in huge slabs, one on top of another as if it had been carved [378] and put under the ground. A camel can carry two slabs of salt. Nobody lives in it except slaves of the Massūfa who dig for the salt and live on dates brought to them from Darʿa and Sijilmāsa, and on the meat of camels, and on *anli* which is brought from the land of the blacks.24 The blacks arrive from their country and carry away the salt from there. A camel load of it is sold in Īwālātan [Walata] for from eight to ten *mithqāls*, and in the town of Māllī for twenty to thirty *mithqāls*, perhaps the price reaches up to forty.25 The blacks exchange the salt as money as one would exchange gold and silver. They cut it up and trade with it in pieces. In spite of the insignificance of the village of Taghāzā, the trading in it comes to the equivalent of many *qinṭars* of gold dust. We stayed in it ten days in miserable condition [379], because its water is bitter and it is of all places the most full of flies. In it water is drawn for the entry into the desert which comes after it. This desert is a travelling distance of ten days and there is no water in it except rarely.[26] But we found much water in it in pools left behind by the rains. One day we found a pool of sweet water between two hillocks of rocks. We quenched our thirst from it and washed our clothes. In that desert truffles are abundant. There are also so many lice in it that people put strings around their necks in which there is mercury which kills the lice. In those days we used to go ahead in front of the caravan. When we found a place suitable for pasture we would let the animals pasture. We did not cease from that practice until a man known as ibn Zīrī was lost in the desert. I did not go ahead after that [380] nor stay behind.

Ibn Zīrī had a quarrel and altercation with the son of his maternal uncle who was called ibn ʿAdī and he stayed behind the company and lost his way. When people dismounted there was no news of him. I advised his cousin to hire someone from the Massūfa to follow his tracks so that he might perhaps find him. He refused. The day after, a man of the Massūfa without payment volunteered to seek him and found his tracks. He had followed the beaten track, sometimes going out of it and sometimes not. He did not find him nor news of him. We met a caravan on the way. They informed us that some men had stayed behind. We found one of them dead under a little tree of the kind that grows in the sand. His clothes were on him and a whip was in his hand. The water was about a mile from him.

Then [381] we arrived at Tāsarahlā where water is exuded by

31

A PANEL OF THE CATALAN MAP
(Drawn by Abraham Cresques in 1375)

KEY TO THE CATALAN MAP

the ground. The caravans dismount there and stay three days. They rest and repair their water-bags and fill them with water. They stitch covers on them as a protection from the wind. From there the *takshif* is sent.[27]

AN ACCOUNT OF THE TAKSHĪF

The *takshif* is the name given to every man of the Massūfa who is hired by the people of the caravan to go ahead to Īwālātan with the letters of the people to their friends there, so as to rent houses for them and to come out to meet them with water a distance of four days. He who has no friend in Īwālātan writes to a person who is known among the merchants of Īwālātan for his generosity and he enters into partnership with him. If perhaps the *takshif* perishes [382] in this desert, then the people of Īwālātan do not know about the caravan, so its people, or most of them, perish.

That desert has many devils, and if the *takshif* be alone, they play with him and lure him on until he loses his way and perishes since there is no way which is clear there and no tracks. There is only sand blown by the wind. You see mountains of sand in a place, then you see they have moved to another. The guide there is a person who has frequented that route and has intelligence. I saw as a remarkable thing that the man who was our guide was blind in one eye and sick in the second. But he was the most knowledgeable of people with regard to the road. We hired the *takshif* on this journey for one hundred *mithqāls* of gold. He was of the Massūfa. On the night of the seventh day we saw the fires of those [383] who came out for our meeting

34

and we were happy about that. This desert is bright, full of sunlight, one's chest is dilated, the soul finds good in it, it is secure from robbers. There are many wild cattle, a herd of them can come so near to people that they can hunt them with dogs and arrows. But their meat when eaten generates a thirst. Many people avoid it because of that. A curious thing about these cattle is that when they are killed water is found in their stomach. I have seen people of the Massūfa pressing the stomach of one of them and drinking the water in it. There are also many serpents in this desert.

AN ANECDOTE

There was in the caravan a merchant of Tilimsān [Tlemcen], known as al Ḥājj Zayyān. It was his custom to seize snakes and play with them. I used to tell him not to [384], but he did not desist. So on another day he put his hand on the hole of a lizard to bring it out. He found in its place a snake. He took hold of it with his hand. He wanted to mount and it bit him on the index finger of the right hand. He was affected by great pain. His hand was cauterized but the pain increased later in the day. He killed a camel and put his hand in its stomach and left it like that all night. Then the flesh of his finger came off and he cut it off at the base. People of the Massūfa told us that that snake must have had a drink of water before biting him; if it had not drunk, it would have killed him.

When those who had come out to meet us arrived with the water, we gave our horses drink and we entered a desert of intense heat, not like the one we were accustomed to. We used

35

to set out after the later afternoon prayer and travel all night, dismounting [385] in the morning. Men from the Massūfa and Bardāma and others would come with loads of water for sale. Then we arrived at the town of Īwālātan [Walata] at the beginning of the month of Rabiʿi al'Awwal after a journey of two whole months from Sijilmāsa. It is the first district of the blacks, and the representative of the sultan in it was Farbā Husain, and the meaning of 'Farbā' is 'the representative'. And when we arrived there, the merchants placed their goods in an open place and the blacks undertook to look after them. They went to the Farba. He was sitting on a mat in a roofed open hall and his helpers were before him with spears and bows in their hands and the elders of the Massūfa behind him. The merchants stood in front of him and he spoke to them through an interpreter in spite of their nearness to him, in derision of them. At that moment I regretted my arrival in their country because of the badness [386] of their manners and their despising of the whites.[28]

I went to the house of ibn Baddāʿ, an excellent man of the people of Salā. I had written to him to rent a house for me and he had done that. Then the Overseer of Īwālātan, whose name was Manshā Jū, invited those who had come in the caravan to his hospitality. I refused to attend that affair, but my friends insisted very much; so I went with the rest. Then the meal was brought out: a concoction of *anli* mixed with a drop of honey and milk, which they placed in a half calabash like a deep wooden bowl. Those present drank and went away. I said to them, 'Was it for this the black invited us?' They said, 'Yes, this is great entertainment in their country.'[29] I became sure

36

then that there was no good to be expected from them. I wanted to travel back with the pilgrims of Īwālātan. [387] Then it seemed good to me to go to see the capital [or: residence, presence] of their King. My residence in Īwālātan was about fifty days. Its people were generous to me and entertained me. Among my hosts was its *qāḍī*, Muḥammad ibn ʿAbd Allāh ibn Yanūmar and his brother, the *faqīh* and teacher Yaḥyā. The town of Īwālātan is very hot and there are in it a few small date palms in whose shade they plant melons. They obtain water from the ground which exudes it. Mutton is obtainable in quantity there. The clothes of its people are of fine Egyptian material. Most of the inhabitants belong to the Massūfa, and as for their women—they are extremely beautiful and are more important than the men.

ANECDOTE CONCERNING THE MASSŪFA WHO INHABIT ĪWĀLĀTAN

The condition of these people [388] is strange and their manners outlandish. As for their men, there is no sexual jealousy in them. And none of them derives his genealogy from his father but, on the contrary, from his maternal uncle. A man does not pass on inheritance except to the sons of his sister to the exclusion of his own sons. Now that is a thing I never saw in any part of the world except in the country of the unbelievers of the land of Mulaībār [Malabar] among the Indians. As to the former [the Massūfa], they are Muslims keeping to the prayers, studying *fiqh* [islamic jurisprudence], and learning the Qur'ān by heart. With regard to their women, they are not modest in the presence

37

of men, they do not veil themselves in spite of their persever-
ance in the prayers.[30] He who wishes to marry among them can
marry, but the women do not travel with the husband, and if
one of them wanted to do that, she would be prevented by her
family. The women there have friends and companions amongst
men outside the prohibited degrees of marriage [i.e., other than
brothers, fathers, etc.]. Likewise for the men, [389] there are
companions from amongst women outside the prohibited degrees. One of them would enter his house to find his wife with
her companion and would not disapprove of that conduct.

ANECDOTE

One day I entered upon the *qāḍi* in Īwālātan after he had given
his permission for me to enter. I found with him a woman—
young in age and very beautiful. When I saw her, I was taken
aback and wanted to retrace my steps. She laughed at me and
was not overcome by modesty. The *qāḍi* said to me, 'Why are
you retreating? She is only my companion.' I was astonished at
their conduct—for he was from the *faqih* class and had performed the pilgrimage. I was informed that he had asked permission of the sultan to go on the pilgrimage that year with his
female companion—I do not know whether she was this one or
not—anyhow, the sultan did not permit him.

[390] AN ANECDOTE LIKE IT
One day I entered upon Abū Muḥammad Yandakān, a man of
the Massūfa, the one in whose company we had arrived. I found

him sitting on a mat and in the middle of his house was a bed with a canopy. On it was a woman and with her a man was sitting, and the two were conversing. I said to him, 'Who is this woman?' He said, 'She is my wife.' I said, 'What is [the relationship of] the man with her to her?' He said, 'He is her companion.' I said, 'Do you accept this when you have lived in our country and have known the matters of the *shar*ᶜ [divine law]?' He said to me, 'Women's companionship with men in our country is honourable and takes place in a good way: there is no suspicion about it. They are not like the women in your country.' I was astonished at his thoughtless answer and I went away from him and did not go to him after this. Though he invited me many times, I did not respond.

When I decided on the journey [391] to Malli which is twenty-four days of travel from Iwālātan for a person who exerts himself, I hired a guide from the Massūfa, since there is no need to travel with companions because of the safety of that road, and went out with three of my friends.[31] That road has many trees which are tall and of great girth: a caravan can find shade in the shadow of one tree; some of them have no branches and no leaves, but the shadow of its trunk is such that a man can find shade in it. Some of those trees have rotted inside and rainwater collects in them. Such a tree is like a well and people drink of the water which is in it. Bees and honey are in some and people extract the honey from the trees. I have passed by one of these trees and found inside it a weaver with his loom set up in it—he was weaving. I was amazed by him. Ibn Juzayy says that in the land of al-Andalus there are two trees of the chestnut type [392] in the hollow trunk of each one of which a weaver weaves clothes. One of them was in the side of the valley of Āsh [Guadix], the other at Bushshāra [Alpuxaras] in Grenada.[32] To resume—in the trees of this forest which is between Īwālātan and Malli, there are trees whose fruits are like those of plums, apples, peaches and apricots, though they are not quite the same as these. There are trees that bear fruit like the cucumber, when it ripens it bursts uncovering something like flour: they cook it and eat it and it is sold in the markets.[33] They dig out from the ground a crop like beans and they fry and eat it. Its taste is like fried peas. Sometimes they grind it and make from it something like a sponge cake, frying it with *gharti*: *gharti* is a fruit like a plum which is very sweet and harmful to white men when they eat it. The hard part inside is crushed and an oil is extracted from it. From this they derive [393] a number of benefits. Amongst these are: they cook with it, fuel the lamps, fry that sponge I mentioned with it, they use it as an ointment, and they mix it with a kind of earth of theirs and plaster the houses with it in the way whitewash is used. Amongst them it is plentiful and easy to come by, and it is carried from one town to another in big calabashes.[34] One of the calabashes is big enough to contain what a large jar would contain in our country. The calabashes in the land of the blacks become big and from them they make wooden dishes. They cut the calabash in two halves and make from it two dishes and they decorate them with beautiful decorations. When one of them travels he is followed by his men and women slaves carrying his bedding and the vessels from which he eats and drinks which are made out of calabashes. The traveller in this land carries neither food nor relishes and no *dīnārs* or *dirhams* [i.e., coins large or small in

40

value]. He only carries [394] slabs of salt and glass trinkets which the people call beads and some perfumery. The things which please them most are cloves, aromatic gums, and *tāsirghant*, which is their incense. When the traveller arrives in a village the women of the blacks come with *anlī* and milk and chickens and flour of *nabaq* [lotus], rice, and *fūnī* [fonio), this is like the grain of mustard and from it *kuskusu* and porridge are made, and bean flour.[35] He buys from them what he likes, but not rice, as eating the rice is harmful to white men and the *fūnī* is better than it.

After a distance of ten days' travel from Īwālātan, we arrived at the village of Zāgharī, which is a big place with black merchants living in it. They are called Wanjarāta, and there live with them a group of white men who follow the sect [395] of the Ibāḍī from amongst the Khārijites. They are called Ṣaghanaghū.[36] The Sunni *māliki* among the white men in that country are called Tūrī.[37] From this town *anlī* is brought to Īwālātan. Then we went from Zāgharī and arrived at the great river, the Nile. On it is the town of Kārsakhū. The Nile descends from it to Kābara, then to Zāgha.[38] Kābara and Zāgha have two sultans who give obedience to the king of Malli. And the people of Zāgha are old in Islam, they are religious and seekers after knowledge.

Then the Nile comes down from Zāgha to Tunbuktū (Timbuktu], then to Kawkaw [Gao], the two places we shall mention below. Then it comes to the town of Mūlī, which is the land of the Līmiyyūn and is the last county of Malli. Then the river flows to Yūfī [Nupe?], which is one of the biggest cities of [396] the blacks. Their sultan is one of their greatest sultans. A white

RUINS OF WALATA

man cannot go there because they would kill him before he arrived there. Then the river comes down from there to the land of the Nubians who follow the Naṣrāniyya [Christian] faith, and on to Dunqula [Dongola], which is the biggest town in their land. Their sultan is called ibn Kanz al-Dīn who became Muslim in the days of al-Malik al-Nāṣir. Then it descends to the cataracts. This is the last district of the blacks and the first of Uswān [Aswan] in Upper Egypt.[39]

I saw a crocodile in this place [i.e., at Kārshkhū] on the Nile near the shore like a small canoe. One day I went down to the Nile to answer a need and one of the blacks came and stood between me and the river. I was astonished at his bad manners and the paucity of his shame. I mentioned that to some one. He answered, 'He only did that for fear on your behalf of danger from the crocodile [397]. He made a barrier between you and it.'

Then we went from Kārsakhū and reached a river called the Ṣanṣara, which is about ten miles from Malli.[40] It is their custom to prevent people entering the city except with permission. I had written beforehand to the white community whose leaders are Muḥammad ibn al-Faqīh al-Juzūlī and Shams al-Din ibn al Naqwīsh, the Egyptian, to rent me a house.

When I arrived at the river just mentioned, I crossed in a ferry and nobody prevented me. I arrived at the city of Malli, the capital of the king of the blacks. I alighted by the graveyard and went to the quarter of the whites. I sought out Muḥammad ibn al-Faqīh and found he had rented a house for me opposite his own. I went to it and his son-in-law, the *faqīh* and the Qur'ān reciter, ʿAbd al-Wāḥid, came with candles and food. Then [398] on the following day there came to me ibn al-Faqīh,

Shams al-Dīn ibn al-Naqwīsh and ʿAli al-Zūdī al-Marrākushī (he is a scholar). I met the *qāḍī* of Malli, ʿAbd al-Rahmān, who came to see me: he is a black, has been on the pilgrimage, and is a noble person with good qualities of character. He sent me a cow as his hospitality gift. I met the interpreter Dūghā, a noble black and a leader of theirs. He sent me a bull. The *faqīh* ʿAbd al-Wāhid sent me two sacks of *fūnī* and a calabash of *ghartī*. Ibn al-Faqīh sent me rice and *fūnī*. Shams al-Din sent me a hospitality gift. They performed their duty towards me [as a guest] most perfectly; may God bless and reward them for their good deeds! Ibn al-Faqīh was married to the daughter of the paternal uncle of the sultan and she used to take care of us with food and other things.

Ten days after our arrival we ate [399] a porridge made from a thing like colocasia called *qāfī*, to them it is preferable over the rest of the food. The following morning we all became ill. We were six in number and one died. I went to Morning Prayer and fainted during it. I asked one of the Egyptians for a laxative medicine. He brought something called *baidar*, made of plant roots, mixed it with aniseed and sugar and beat it up in water. I drank it and vomited up what I had eaten with a lot of bile. And God preserved me from destruction, but I was sick for two months.

AN ACCOUNT OF THE SULTAN OF MALLI, MANSĀ SULAIMĀN[41]

The sultan of Malli is sultan Mansā Sulaimān: 'Mansā' means 'sultan', and Sulaimān is his name. He is a miserly king, not much giving is to be expected from him. It happened [400] that I stayed this period and did not see him because of my sickness. Then he made food on the occasion of the period of mourning for our Lord Abū'l'Ḥasan (may God be pleased with him!).42 He invited the *amīrs* and *faqīhs* and the *qāḍi* and the *khaṭīb* [preacher], and I attended with them. They brought reading stools and the Qur'ān was read through completely. They prayed for our Lord Abū'l Ḥasan (may God have mercy on him), and for Mansā Sulaimān. When they had finished this I came forward and greeted Mansā Sulaimān. The *qāḍi* and the preacher and ibn al-Faqīh told him about my condition. He answered in their tongue and they said to me, 'The sultan says to you "Thank God".' I said, 'Praise to God and thanks in every situation.'

ANECDOTE CONCERNING THEIR INSIGNIFICANT
HOSPITALITY AND THEIR OSTENTATION CONCERNING IT

When I went [back to my lodgings] a hospitality gift was sent to me and it was directed to the house of the *qāḍi*. He sent it [401] with his men to the house of ibn al-Faqīh. The latter came out from his house in a hurry with bare feet. He entered my house and said, 'Stand up, the sultan's stuff and his present have come for you.' I stood up, thinking they were robes of honour and things of value. But behold—they were three circular pieces of bread, a piece of beef fried in *ghartī*, and a calabash of sour milk. When I saw them, I laughed and wondered a lot at their weakness of mind and their magnifying of the insignificant.

I stayed after the sending of this hospitality gift two months, during which nothing reached me from the sultan. Then came the month of Ramaḍān. Meanwhile I had been going frequently to [402] the place of audience [*mashwar*], greeting him and sitting with the *qāḍī* and the preacher. I had a word with Dūghā, the interpreter. He said, 'Speak before him and I will express on your behalf what is necessary.' At a session at the beginning of Ramaḍān, I stood before the sultan and said to him, 'I have indeed travelled in the lands of the world. I have met their kings. I have been in your country four months and you have given me no hospitality and have not given me anything. What shall I say about you before the sultans?' He said, 'Indeed, I have not seen you nor did I know about you.' The *qāḍī* and ibn al-Fāqīh got up and answered him saying, 'He has greeted you and you sent him food.' Then the sultan ordered a house for me in which I stayed and he fixed an allowance for me. Then he shared out money among the *qāḍī*, the preacher and the men of *fiqh* on the night of the twenty-seventh of Ramaḍān. They call it the *zakāt*.[43] He gave me a share with them of thirty-three and a third *mithqāls*. He was gracious to me at my departure, to the extent of giving me one hundred *mithqāls* of gold.

[403] AN ACCOUNT OF THE SULTAN'S SITTING IN HIS
    CUPOLA

The sultan has a raised cupola which is entered from inside his house. He sits in it a great part of the time. It has on the audience side a chamber with three wooden arches, the woodwork is

46

covered with sheets of beaten silver and beneath these, three more covered with beaten gold, or, rather, it is silver covered with gilt. The windows have woollen curtains which are raised on a day when the sultan will be in session in his cupola: thus it is known that he is holding a session. When he sits, a silken cord is put out from the grill of one of the arches with a scarf of Egyptian embroidery tied to it. When the people see the scarf, drums are beaten and bugles sounded. Then from the door of the palace come out about three hundred slaves. Some have bows in their hands and some small spears and shields. Some of the spearmen stand on the right and some on the left, the bowmen sit [404] likewise. Then they bring two mares saddled and bridled, and with them two rams. They say that these are effective against the evil eye. When the sultan has sat down three of his slaves go out quickly to call his deputy, Qanjā Mūsā. The *farāriyya* [commanders] arrive, and they are the *amīrs* [officers], and among them are the preacher and the men of *fiqh*, who sit in front of the armed men on the right and left of the place of audience. The interpreter Dūghā stands at the door of the audience chamber wearing splendid robes of *zardkhāna* and others.[44] On his head is a turban which has fringes, they have a superb way of tying a turban. He is girt with a sword whose sheath is of gold, on his feet are light boots and spurs. And nobody wears boots that day except he. In his hands there are two small spears, one of gold and one of silver with points of iron. The soldiers, the district governors, the pages and the Massūfa and others are seated [405] outside the place of audience in a broad street which has trees in it.[45] Each *farārī* [commander] has his followers before him with their spears, bows, drums and bugles made of elephant tusks. Their instruments of music are made of reeds and calabashes, and they beat them with sticks and produce a wonderful sound. Each *farārī* has a quiver which he places between his shoulders. He holds his bow in his hand and is mounted on a mare. Some of his men are on foot and some on mounts.

Inside the audience chamber under the arches a man is standing; he who wants to speak to the sultan speaks to Dūg̲h̲ā, Dūg̲h̲ā speaks to the man who is standing, and he speaks to the sultan.

√AN ACCOUNT OF THE SESSIONS IN THE PLACE OF AUDIENCE

The sultan sits on certain days in the palace yard to give audience. There is a platform under a tree with three steps which they call *banbī*.[46] [406] It is covered with silk and has pillows placed on it. The *shaṭr* is raised, this is a shelter made of silk with a golden bird like a sparrowhawk above it.[47] The sultan comes out from a gate in the corner of the palace, bow in hand, his quiver between his shoulders, and on his head a cap of gold tied with a golden band which has fringes like thin-bladed knives more than a span long. He often wears a robe which is soft and red, made from Roman cloth called *muṭanfas*.[48] The singers go out before him carrying gold and silver *qanābir*[49] and behind him come three hundred armed slaves. The sultan walks slowly and pauses often and sometimes he stops completely. When he comes to the *banbī* he stops and looks at the people. Then he mounts the steps with dignity in the manner of

48

a preacher getting into the pulpit. [407] When he sits down they beat the drums, blow the bugles and the horns, and three of the slaves go out in haste and call the deputy and the *farāriyya* [commanders]. They enter and sit down. The two mares are brought in with the two rams. Dūg̱ẖā stands at the door while the rest of the people are in the street under the tree.

AN ACCOUNT OF THE SELF-ABASEMENT OF THE BLACKS BEFORE THEIR KING, THEIR DUSTING THEMSELVES FOR HIM, AND OTHER PECULIAR THINGS

The blacks are the most humble of men before their king and the most extreme in their self-abasement before him. They swear by his name, saying, 'Mansā Sulaimānkī' [the law of Mansā Sulaimān]. When he calls one of them while he is in session in his cupola which we described above, the man invited takes off his clothes and wears patched clothes, takes off his turban, puts on a dirty cap, and goes in [408] raising his clothes and trousers up his legs half-way to his knees. He advances with humility looking like a beggar. He hits the ground with his elbows, he hits it hard. He stands bowed, like one in the *rukuʿ* position in prayer, listening to what the king says. When one of them speaks to the sultan and he gives him an answer, he removes his clothes from his back and throws dust on his head and back, as a person does when bathing with water. I used to wonder how they do not blind their eyes. When the sultan speaks in his council, at his word those present take their turbans off their heads and listen to the speech.

Sometimes one of them would stand before him and recall

49

what he had done in his service, saying, 'I did such and such on such a day,' and, 'I killed so and so on such a day.' Those who know this confirm that he is telling the truth. Their confirmation is by pulling the strings of their bows and letting them go, as one does when one is shooting. If the sultan says to him that he has spoken the truth [409] or thanks him, he takes off his clothes and dusts. This is good manners among them.

Ibn Juzzayy says:

I have been informed by a keeper of the seal, the *faqīh*, Abū al-Qāsim, son of Riḍwān (may Allah strengthen him!) that when al-Ḥājj Mūsa the Wanjarātī came as ambassador from Mansā Sulaimān to our lord Abū al-Ḥasan (may Allah be pleased with him!)—when he entered the Noble Assembly, one of his men carried with him a round basket and he dusted every time our lord said a gracious word to him as he would in his own country.[50]

10 AN ACCOUNT OF WHAT THE SULTAN DOES AT THE ʿID PRAYERS AND THEIR ACCOMPANYING DAYS

I was present at Malli for two festivals—the Feast of Sacrifices and the Feast of Fast-breaking.[51] The people came out to the Place of Prayer which is near the sultan's [410] palace wearing good white clothes. The sultan was riding: he had the *ṭailasān* on his head, and the blacks do not wear the *ṭailasān* except at festivals, although the *qāḍi* and the preacher and the *faqīhs* do indeed wear this headdress on other days.[52] On a festival day they precede the sultan and declare the oneness and greatness of God.[53] Before the sultan are carried red banners made of silk. Near the Place of Prayer a tent has been set up. The sultan goes

50

WEST AFRICAN MOSQUE OF THE 14TH CENTURY IN TIMBUKTU

into it, puts himself in order, then he comes out to the Place of Prayer, the prayer is performed and a sermon delivered. The preacher comes down from the pulpit and sits down before the sultan. He makes a long speech. There is there a man with a spear in his hand who explains the things said by the preacher to the people in their tongue. The speech is made up of exhortation, reminders [of the hereafter], praise for the sultan, encouragement to remain obedient, and to give respect as is appropriate.[54]

The sultan holds sessions [411] during the days associated with the two festivals after the ʿasr [late afternoon] prayers on the banbi.[55] The men-at-arms come with wonderful weaponry: quivers of silver and gold, swords covered with gold, their sheaths of the same, spears of silver and gold and wands of crystal. Four of the amīrs stand behind him to drive off flies, with ornaments of silver in their hands which look like riding stirrups. The farāriyya [commanders], the qāḍī, and the preacher sit according to custom, the interpreter Dūghā brings in his four wives and his concubines, who are about a hundred in number. On them are fine clothes and on their heads they have bands of silver and gold with silver and gold apples as pendants. A chair is set there for Dūghā to sit on and he beats an instrument which is made of reeds [412] with tiny calabashes below it, praising the sultan, recalling in his song his expeditions and deeds.[56] The wives and the concubines sing with him and they play with bows. There are with them about thirty of his pages wearing red woollen robes and white caps on their heads. Each one of them has a drum tied to him and he beats it. Then come his retinue of young men who play and turn in the air as they

52

do in Sind. They have a wonderful gracefulness and lightness in this. They juggle with swords beautifully and Dūghā performs a marvellous game with the sword. At that point, the sultan orders that a gift be given him, they bring him a purse of two hundred *mithqāls* of gold dust. An announcement of its contents is made to him over the heads of the people. The *farāriyya* [commanders] get up and twang their bows, thanking the sultan.

On the following day every one of them makes a gift to Dūghā [413] according to his means. Every Friday after the ʿasr prayer Dūghā performs ceremonies like those which we have recounted.

AN ACCOUNT OF THE LAUGHABLE MANNER IN WHICH THEIR POETS HOLD A RECITATION

When it is a festival day and Dūghā has completed his play, the poets called the *julāʾ* (and the singular is *jālī*) come.[57] Each one of them has got inside a costume made of feathers to look like a thrush with a wooden head made for it and a red beak as if it were the head of a bird. They stand before the sultan in that ridiculous attire and recite their poetry. It was mentioned to me that their poetry is a kind of preaching. In it they tell the sultan that this *banbī* on which he is, such and such of the kings of Malli sat on it [414], and such and such were the good deeds of one, and such and such another's. 'So do good, that good will be recounted after you.' Then the Archpoet mounts the steps of the *banbī* and places his head on the sultan's lap. Then he climbs to the top of the *banbī* and places it on his right shoulder, then on the left, meanwhile speaking in their tongue; thereupon

53

he comes down. I was informed that this performance is old amongst them; they continued it from before Islam.

AN ANECDOTE

I was present in the audience of the sultan one day when there came one of their *faqīhs*. He had arrived from a distant district. He stood up before the sultan and spoke many words. The *qāḍī* got up and confirmed his words and the two of them were confirmed by the sultan. Everyone of them took off his turban from his head and dusted before him. There was [415] next to me a man who said to me, 'Do you know what they said?' I said, 'I do not know.' He said:

> 'The *faqīh* reported that locusts fell on their land. One of their pious men went out to the place where the locusts were. He was frightened by their quantity. He said, "This is too great a number of locusts." One of the locusts answered him, "Truly there is too great wrong in the land, God sends us to spoil that which is planted." The *qāḍī* confirmed his statement and so did the sultan. He said to the *amīrs* [officers], "I am innocent of wrong, him who commits wrong amongst you, I shall punish. The man who knows about a wrongdoer and does not inform me about him, the crime of that wrongdoer is upon him, and God will be his reckoner and interrogator." When he uttered this statement, the *farāriyya* [commanders] took off their turbans from their heads and declared their innocence from wrongdoing.[58]

AN ANECDOTE

[416] Another time I was present at the Friday prayers. There stood up one of the merchants from among the scholars of the

Massūfa. His name was Abū Ḥafṣ. He said, 'O people of the mosque, I make you witnesses to the case I have against Mansā Sulaimān before the Apostle of God (may God grant him grace and peace!)' When he said that there came out to him a group of men from the *maqṣūra* [sovereign's enclosure] of the sultan. They asked him, 'Who wronged you, who has taken anything from you?' He said, '*Mansha* Jū of Īwālātan,' that is, the governor, 'he took from me what is valued at six hundred *mithqāls*. He wanted to give me as its value only one hundred *mithqāls*.' The sultan sent for him. As soon as he appeared after some days he sent them both to the *qāḍī* who confirmed the merchant's right and he took the award. After that the governor was removed from his work.

AN ANECDOTE

[417] It came about in the days of my stay in Malli that the sultan was angry with his senior wife, the daughter of his paternal uncle, who was called Qāsā which signifies the queen among them. The queen is his partner in the kingship, following the custom of the blacks. Her name is mentioned with his in the pulpit.[59]

The sultan imprisoned the queen in the house of one of the *farāriyya* [commanders] and appointed in her place his other wife, Banjū. She was not from among the daughters of the kings. The people discussed this a lot and disapproved of the action. The daughters of his paternal uncle visited Banjū to congratulate her on her queenship. They placed ashes on their arms but did not dust their heads. Then the sultan released

55

Qāsā from her bonds. The daughters of his paternal uncle visited her to congratulate her on her release and they dusted as is customary. Banjū complained to the sultan about this. [418] He became angry with the daughters of his paternal uncle and they were afraid of him and took refuge in the congregational Mosque. He forgave them and called them back. It is their custom when they go in to the sultan to strip themselves of their clothes and enter naked. They did this and he pardoned them. They then took to coming to the door of the sultan morning and evening for a period of seven days—as anyone does who is pardoned by the sultan. And Qāsā took to riding every day at the head of her slave girls and slaves with dust on their heads. She stopped by the place of audience covering her head, and nothing being seen but her face. The *amīrs* [officers] spoke much about her affair. The sultan gathered them to the place of audience and Dūghā said on his behalf, 'You have spoken a great deal concerning the matter of Qāsā, but she has committed a great crime.' Then he brought a slave woman of hers, fettered and shackled. She was ordered to tell what she knew. She reported that [419] Qāsā had sent her to Jaṭal, the son of the paternal uncle of the sultan, who had escaped him and gone to Kanburnī, to call him to dethrone the sultan from his kingdom.[60] And she said to him, 'I and all the askaris are under your orders.' When the *amīrs* [officers] heard this they said, 'This is a great crime and she deserves death for it.' Qāsā was afraid because of this and took refuge in the house of the preacher. It was their custom to take refuge in the mosque and if that were not possible, in the house of the preacher.

The blacks used to hate Mansā Sulaimān because of his

miserliness. Before him there was Mansā Maghā, and before Mansā Maghā, Mansā Mūsā. He was generous and noble and loved the white men and was kind to them. He is the one who gave Abū Isḥāq al-Sāḥilī in one day four thousand *mithqāls*. I was informed by a reliable person that he gave Mudrik ibn Faqqūṣ three thousand [420] *mithqāls* in one day—his grandfather Sāraq Jāṭa had been made a Muslim by the hand of the grandfather of this Mudrik.61

AN ANECDOTE 14

I was informed by this Mudrik the *faqīh* that a man from the people of Tilimsān [Tlemcen] known as ibn Shaikh al-Laban had been kind to the sultan Mansā Mūsā in his childhood, by giving him seven and one third *mithqāls*. He was then a young boy, not taken much notice of. Then it happened he came to him while he was sultan about a case. He recognized him and invited him forward and brought him near to himself so that he sat with him on the *banbī*. He then recalled what he had done for him. He said to his *amīrs* [officers], 'What is the reward for him who has done the good which he has done?' They said to him, 'For a good deed, ten like it. Give him seventy *mithqāls*.'62 The sultan thereupon gave him seven hundred *mithqāls*, a robe of honour, slaves and servants [421] and ordered him to visit him often. I was told this story also by the son of ibn Shaikh al-Laban whom I have mentioned; this son was a scholar teaching the Qur'ān at Malli.

Amongst their good qualities is the small amount of injustice amongst them, for of all people they are the furthest from it. Their sultan does not forgive anyone in any matter to do with injustice. Among these qualities there is also the prevalence of peace in their country, the traveller is not afraid in it nor is he who lives there in fear of the thief or of the robber by violence. They do not interfere with the property of the white man who dies in their country even though it may consist of great wealth, but rather they entrust it to the hand of someone dependable among the white men until it is taken by the rightful claimant.

Another of the good habits amongst them is [422] the way they meticulously observe the times of the prayers and attendance at them, so also it is with regard to their congregational services and their beating of their children to instill these things in them.[63]

When it is Friday, if a man does not come early to the mosque he will not find a place to pray because of the numbers of the crowd. It is their custom for every man to send his boy with his prayer mat. He spreads it for him in a place commensurate with his position and keeps the place until he comes to the mosque. Their prayer-mats are made of the leaves of a tree like a date palm but it bears no fruit.

Among their good qualities is their putting on of good white clothes on Friday. If a man among them has nothing except a tattered shirt, he washes and cleans it and attends the Friday prayer in it. Another of their good qualities is their concern for learning the sublime Qur'ān by heart. They make fetters for their children when they appear on their part to be falling short in their learning of it by heart, and they are not taken off from them till they do learn by heart. I went in to visit the *qāḍī* on an 'Id day and his children [423] were tied up. I said to him, 'Why do you not release them?' He said, 'I shall not do so until they learn the Qur'ān by heart.' One day I passed by a handsome youth from them dressed in fine clothes and on his feet was a heavy chain. I said to the man who was with me, 'What has this youth done—has he killed someone?' The youth heard my remark and laughed. It was told me, 'He has been chained so that he will learn the Qur'ān by heart.'

Among the bad things which they do—their serving women, slave women and little daughters appear before people naked, exposing their private parts. I used to see many of them in this state in Ramaḍān, for it was the custom of the *farāriyya* [commanders] to break the fast in the sultan's house. Everyone of them has his food carried in to him by twenty or more of his slave girls and they are naked, every one. Also among their bad customs is the way women will go [424] into the presence of the sultan naked, without any covering; and the nakedness of the sultan's daughters—on the night of the twenty-seventh of Ramaḍān, I saw about a hundred slave girls coming out of his palace with food, with them were two of his daughters, they had full breasts and no clothes on. Another of their bad customs is their putting of dust and ashes on their heads as a sign of respect. And another is the laughing matter I mentioned of their poetic recitals. And another is that many of them eat animals not ritually slaughtered, and dogs and donkeys.

My entry into Malli was on the fourteenth of the first month of Jumādā in the year '53 [i.e., 753 A.H., 28th June A.D. 1352], and my going out from there was on the twenty-second of Muḥarram in the year '54 [i.e., 754 A.H., 27 February A.D. 1353]. I was accompanied by a merchant known as Abū [425] Bakr ibn Yaʿqūb. We set out on the Mīma road. I was riding a camel because horses were dear, costing about one hundred *mithqāls* apiece. We reached a large arm of the river which comes out of the Nile and which cannot be crossed except in boats. That place has many mosquitoes and nobody passes through except at night.[64] We arrived at the arm of the river in the first third of the night and it was moonlight.

NOTE ON THE HORSES WHICH ARE IN THE NILE

When we arrived at the arm of the river, I saw on its bank sixteen beasts with enormous bodies. I was astonished by them. I thought they were elephants because there are plenty there. Then I saw them entering the river and said to Abū Bakr ibn Yaʿqūb, 'What beasts are these?' He said, 'These are horses of the river [hippopotami], they have come out [426] to graze on the dry land.' They are more thickset than horses and they have manes and tails, their heads are like the heads of horses and their legs like the legs of elephants. I saw these horses another time when we were travelling on the Nile from Tunbuktū to Kawkaw; they were swimming in the water and raising their heads and blowing. The boatmen feared them and came in close to the shore so as not to be drowned by them. They have a nice trick in hunting them, that is, they have spears with holes in them and put strong cords through these holes. They hit the horse with them; if by any chance the throw gets the foot or the neck, it goes through it and they pull him by the rope until they bring him to the bank. They kill him and eat his meat. There are great heaps of their bones on the river bank.

When we dismounted we stayed by this arm of the river in a large village ruled by a black governor who was a *hajji* and a gentleman and was called Farbā Maghā. [427] He was one of those who had made the pilgrimage with sultan Mansā Musā when he made his pilgrimage.[65]

AN ANECDOTE

I was told by Farbā Māghā that when Mansā Musā arrived at this branch of the river there was with him a *qāḍī*, a white man, whose *kunya* was Abū 'l-ʿAbbās, he was also known as al-Dukkālī [man of the Dukkāla tribe in Morocco]. The sultan gave him as a present four thousand *mithqāls* for his expenses. When they arrived at Mīma he complained to the sultan that the four thousand *mithqāls* had been stolen from him from his house. The sultan caused the *amīr* of Mīma to appear and threatened him with death if he did not present the man who stole the money. The *amīr* sought the thief and did not find anyone, for there are no thieves in their country. He entered the house of the *qāḍī* and was violent with his servants and threatened them. One of his slave girls said to him, 'He lost nothing, he only buried it [428] with his own hand in that place.' She pointed to the place. The *amīr* removed the gold and brought it to the

61

sultan and told him the story. He was angry with the *qāḍī* and exiled him to the country of the unbelievers who eat human beings. He stayed among them four years. Then the sultan sent him back to his own country. The reason that he was not eaten by the unbelievers was his whiteness for they say that eating a white man is harmful because he is not ripe. The black man however is ripe according to them.[66]

AN ANECDOTE

There came to sultan Mansā Sulaimān a group of these blacks who eat human beings accompanied by one of their *amīrs*. According to their custom they had put in their ears large rings each of which was a span and a half across. They cover themselves in silk mantles. In their country there is a gold [429] mine. The sultan was gracious to them. He gave them as a hospitality gift a slave woman. They slaughtered her and ate her. They smeared their faces and hands with her blood and came to the sultan to return thanks. I was told that it is their custom to do that whenever they come to visit him. It was mentioned to me concerning them that they say that the tastiest meat in the flesh of women is the palm and the breast.

Then we departed from this village which is by the branch of the river I mentioned, and we arrived at the town of Qurī Mansa [or: the built up area of the villages of Mansa]. There my camel which I was riding died. When I was told by its keeper I came out to look at it. I found the blacks had eaten it as their custom is in eating a dead animal. I sent the two boys I had hired to serve me to buy me a camel at Zāgharī which was a

62

distance of about two days' journey. Some of the friends of Abū
Bakr son of Yaᶜqūb stayed with me while the latter went ahead
to receive us [430] at Mīma. I stayed there [Qurī Mansa] for six
days and was entertained by one of the pilgrims in this town
until the two boys arrived with the camel.

AN ANECDOTE

In the days of my stay in this town I had a dream one night in
which a person was saying to me, 'O Muḥammad, son of
Baṭṭūṭa, why do you not read *sūra yāsīn* every day?' From that
day I did not cease to read it every day whether I was travelling
or remaining stationary.[67] Then I departed for the town of
Mīma; in its neighbourhood we dismounted by some wells. We
travelled then from there to the city of Tunbuktū, which is four
miles from the Nile. Most of its inhabitants are Massūfa, people
of the veil. Its governor is called Farbā Mūsā. I was present
with him one day when he appointed [431] one of the Massūfa
as *amīr* over a company. He placed on him a garment, a turban
and trousers, all of them of dyed material. He then seated him
on a shield and he was lifted up by the elders of his tribe on
their heads. In this town is the grave of the unsurpassable poet
Abū ᶜIshāq al-Saḥilī of Gharnāta [Grenada], who is known in
his own country as al-Ṭuwaijin.[68] There also is the grave of
Sirāj al-Dīn ibn al-Ṭūwaik, one of the great merchants from
among the people of Alexandria.

When sultan Mansa Mūsā made the pilgrimage, he stayed in a garden belonging to this Sirāj al-Dīn at Birkat al-Ḥabash [the Ethiopian's Pool] outside Cairo. The sultan lodged there and ran short of money. He borrowed it from Sirāj al-Dīn, and his *amīrs* also borrowed from him. Sirāj al-Dīn sent his representative with them to receive the money, but he stayed in Malli. [432] Then Sirāj al-Dīn himself went to get his money, accompanied by his son. When he reached Tunbuktū he was entertained by Abū ʿIsḥāq al-Saḥilī. It was fate that his death should come that night, and people talked about it, for they suspected that he was poisoned. His son said to them, 'I have eaten that food with him—that very same food. If there were poison in it we would all of us have been killed. But his allotted term had been completed.' His son arrived at Malli, received his money, and went back to Egypt.

At Tunbuktū I embarked on the Nile in a small vessel carved from one piece of wood. We used to come ashore every night in a village to buy what we needed of food and ghee in exchange for salt and perfumes and glass ornaments. Then I reached a town whose name I have been caused [by Satan] to forget. This town had as its *amīr* an excellent man, a pilgrim called Farbā Sulaimān, well known for his bravery and tenacity, no one was able [433] to bend his bow. I did not see among the blacks anyone taller than he nor more massive in body. In this town I needed some millet. I came to him on the birthday of the Apostle of God (may Allah grant him mercy and peace!).[69] I greeted him and he asked me about my arrival. There was with him a *faqīh* who was his scribe. I took a writing board which

64

was before him and wrote on it, 'O *faqīh*, tell this *amīr* that we need some millet for our provisions. Greetings!' I handed over the board to the *faqīh* to read what was written on it privately and to speak to the *amīr* about it in his language. But he read it aloud and the *amīr* understood it. He took me by the hand and made me enter his audience room. In its were many weapons: shields, bows and spears. I found in his house a copy of the *kitāb al-mudhish* [the Book of the Astonishing] of ibn al-Jawzī, [434] and I began to read it.[70] Then a drink of theirs called *daqnū* was served. It is water with pounded millet mixed with a little honey or milk in it. They drink it instead of water, because if they drink the water by itself, it harms them.[71] If they have no millet, they mix it with honey or milk. Then a green melon was served and we ate from it.

A growing boy came in; the governor called him and said to me, 'Here is your hospitality gift. Guard him so that he does not run away.'[72] I took him and I wanted to turn away. He said, 'Stay till food is served.' An Arab slave girl of his from Damascus came in to us. She was an Arab and spoke to me in Arabic.

While we were in that place, we heard a loud crying in his house. He sent the slave girl to find out the news. She returned to him and informed him that a daughter of his had just died. He said, 'I do not [435] like mourning. Come, let us walk to the river,' meaning the Nile. He had houses on its banks. He brought out a mare and said to me, 'Ride!' But I said, 'I will not ride while you walk.' We walked together and reached his houses on the Nile. He brought out food and we ate. I bade him farewell and went away. I did not see among the blacks a person more generous or better than he. The boy he gave me is still with me up till now.

Then I travelled to the city of Kawkaw [Gao]. It is a big city on the Nile, one of the best of the cities of the blacks. It is one of the biggest and most fertile of their places, with much rice, milk, chicken and fish. In it there are ⁱnānī pumpkins which have no rivals. The transactions of its people in buying and selling are carried out by means of cowries—as is the case among the people of Malli.[73] I stayed there about a month and was the guest of [436] Muḥammad ibn ʿUmar of the people of Miknāsa. He was a gentle person, fond of making jokes, a man of merit.[74] He died there after I left. I was also the guest there of *al-Ḥājj* Muḥammad al-Wajdī al-Tāzī who had travelled to Yaman, and of the *faqīh* Muḥammad al-Fīlālī, *imām* of the mosque of the whites.

Then I travelled from there in the direction of Takaddā [Takidda] in the hinterland [that is, away from the river] with a large caravan of the men of Ghadāmas [Ghadames in Libya] whose guide and leader was *al-Ḥājj* Wujjīn (the meaning of this word is 'jackal' in the language of the blacks).

I had a camel for riding and a she-camel for carrying provisions. When we set out on the first stage the she-camel broke down. *Al-Ḥājj* Wujjīn took what was on her and divided it among his companions. They shared out the burden. There was in the caravan a Maghribin [man of Arab north-west Africa] of the people of Tādalā who refused to carry any of it in the way other people had done. My servant lad was thirsty one day [437], I asked the Maghribin for water; he did not give it.

Then we arrived at the land of the Bardama people [a Tuareg

group], a tribe of the Berbers. The caravan cannot travel except under their protection; and amongst them the protection of a woman is more important than that of a man. They are nomads, they do not stay in one place. Their dwelling places are strange in form: they set up poles of wood and place mats around them, over that they put interwoven sticks and over them skins or cotton cloth. Their women are the most perfect of women in beauty and the most comely in figure, in addition to being pure white and fat. I did not see in the land anyone who attained to their standard of fatness. These women's food is cow's milk and pounded millet; they drink it mixed with water, uncooked, morning and evening. A man who wants to marry among them has to settle with them in the country near [438] them, and not take his spouse further than either Kawkaw or Īwalātan.

I was affected by sickness in this country because of extreme heat, being overcome by yellow bile. We exerted ourselves in travelling till we reached the city of Takaddā. There I lodged in the vicinity of the shaikh of the Maghribins, Saʿīd ibn ʿAlī al-Jazūlī. I was entertained by its *qāḍī*, Abū Ibrāhīm ʿIshāq al-Jānātī, an eminent person. I was also the guest of Jaʿfar ibn Muḥammad al-Massūfī. The houses of Takaddā are built of red stone. Its water supply flows over the copper mines and its colour and taste are changed by that fact. There is no cultivation there except a little wheat which is eaten by the merchants and visitors. It is sold at the rate of twenty of their *mudds* for a *mithqāl* of gold.[75] Their *mudd* is a third of the *mudd* in our country. Millet amongst them is sold at the rate of ninety *mudds* for a gold *mithqāl*. It is a country with many [439] scorpions. Its scorpions kill a child who has not reached puberty, whereas they

rarely kill a man.[76] One day while I was there a scorpion stung a
son of skaikh Sa'īd ibn 'Alī in the morning. He died immediately and I attended his funeral [lit.: the carrying of the
bier].

The people of Takaddā carry on no business but trading.
Every year they travel to Egypt and bring from there everything there is in the country by way of fine cloths and other
things. For its people ease of life and ample condition are
supreme; they vie with one another in the number of slaves and
servants they have—as likewise do the people of Malli and
Īwālātan. They do not sell educated women-slaves, except very
rarely and at a great price.

AN ANECDOTE

When I reached Takaddā I wanted to buy an educated woman-
slave. I could not find one, then the *qāḍī*, Abū Ibrāhīm, sent me
a slave-woman belonging to one of his friends.[77] [440] I bought
her for twenty-five *mithqāls*. Then her master regretted the
transaction and desired to cancel the sale. I said to him, 'If you
direct me to another, I shall cancel the sale.' He directed me to a
slave-woman of 'Alī 'Aghyūl, who was the Maghribin from
Tādallā who refused to transport any part of my luggage when
my she-camel failed me, and refused to give a drink of water to
my servant lad when he was thirsty. I bought her from him—
she was better than the first woman I had bought and I cancelled the sale for my first friend. Then the Maghribin regretted
having sold the slave-woman and desired a cancellation of the
sale. He persisted in it; I refused so as to pay him back for his

evil deed. He almost went mad or was about to perish out of grief. In the end, I cancelled the sale for him.

A NOTE ON THE COPPER MINE

There is a copper mine outside Takaddā. The people dig [441] for it in the earth, bring it to the town, and smelt it in their houses. This is done by their men, and the women-slaves. When they have smelted it into red copper, they make it into rods about the length of a span and a half: some are of fine gauge and some thick. The thick are sold at the rate of four hundred rods for a *mithqāl* of gold, the fine for six or seven hundred to the *mithqāl*: it is their means of exchange. They buy meat and firewood with the fine rods: they buy male and female slaves, millet, ghee, and wheat with the thick. Copper is carried from there to the city of Kūbar [Gobīr] in the land of the unbelievers, to Zaghay and to the country of Barnū (Bornu) which is at a distance of forty days from Takaddā. Its people are Muslim; they have a king whose name is Idrīs, who does not appear before the people nor speak to them except from behind a curtain.[78] From this country are brought [442] beautiful slave women and eunuchs and heavy fabrics. Copper is also taken from Takaddā to Jūjūwat and to the land of the Mūrtibīn and to other places.

ANECDOTE CONCERNING THE SULTAN OF TAKADDĀ

In the days of my stay in that place, the *qāḍī* Abū Ibrāhīm and the preacher Muḥammad and the teacher Abū Ḥafs and the shaikh Sa'īd ibn 'Alī set out to call upon the sultan of Takaddā who was a Berber named Izār, and was at a distance of a day's journey from the town. A dispute had occurred between him and the Takarkurī who is also a sultan of the Berbers. The gentlemen I mentioned had gone to arbitrate between the two of them. I wanted to meet the sultan, so I hired a guide and set out towards him. He was informed by those gentlemen about my arrival and he came to me riding a mare without a saddle [443] as was their custom. In place of a saddle he had a fine red carpet. He had on a mantle, trousers, and a turban which were all blue. With him were the sons of his sister (they are those who will inherit his kingdom). We stood up for him and shook hands with him. He asked after my health and about my arrival, and was informed about these things. He lodged me in one of the houses of the Yanātibūn (they are like the domestic servants at home). He sent me a goat roasted on a spit and a wooden bowl of fresh cow's milk. Nearby to us was the tent of his mother and his sister and the two of them came and greeted us. His mother sent us fresh milk after dusk, which is their milking time. They drink it at that time and in the morning; but as to [normal] food, they do not eat it nor know of it. I stayed there six days and every day he sent two roast sheep—one in the morning and one in the evening. He was gracious to me in giving me [444] a she-camel and ten *mithqāls* of gold. Then I left him and returned to Takaddā.

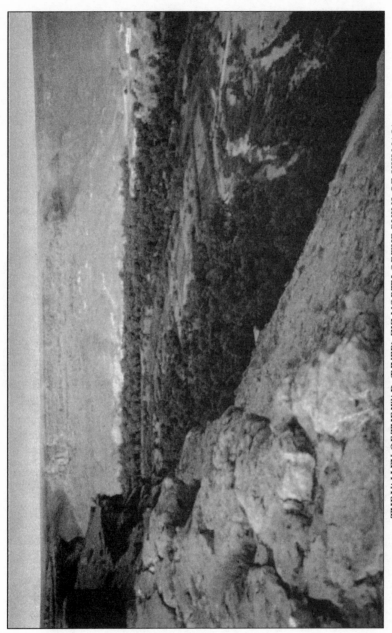

THE VALLEY OF THE WAD (RIVER) ZIZ NORTH OF THE RUINS OF SIJILMASA
(Photo by Ross E. Dunn)

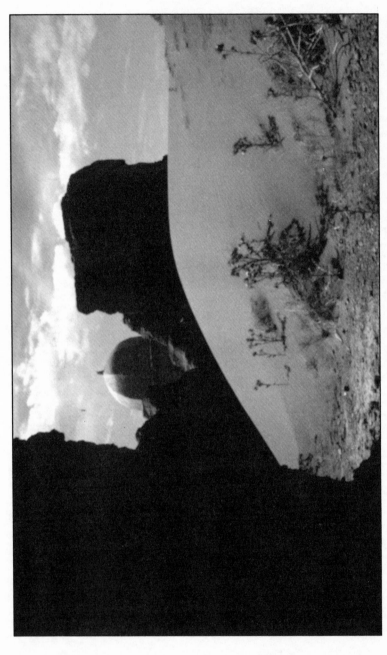

RUINS OF THE OLD CITY FROM WHICH IBN BATTUTA SET OUT ON HIS CAMEL CARAVAN JOURNEY TO MALI. THESE WALLS WERE BUILT SOME CENTURIES AFTER HIS TRAVELS, BUT THIS WAS THE SITE OF THE 14TH CENTURY CITY

(photo by Ross E. Dunn)

When I returned to Takaddā, the young slave of *al-Ḥājj* Muḥammad ibn Saʿīd of Sijilmāsa arrived with a command from our master the commander of the faithful, the supporter of the faith, the depender on the Lord of the worlds, commanding me to appear in his sublime presence. I kissed the order and complied with it immediately. I bought two camels for my riding for thirty-seven and a third *mithqāls*. I wanted to travel to Tuwāt. I carried provisions for seventy nights since [normal] food is not to be found between Takaddā and Tuwāt, only meat and milk and ghee which are bought in exchange for cloth. I left Takaddā on Thursday, the eleventh of Shaʿbān in the year [445] 'fifty-four [A.H. 754; 11th September A.D. 1353] in a big caravan which included Jaʿfar al-Tuwātī, who is an eminent person, and the *faqīh* Muḥammad ibn ʿAbd Allāh, *qāḍī* of Takaddā. In the caravan there were about six hundred slave-women.[79] We arrived at Kāhir in the land of the sultan of Karkarī. It is a land of plentiful grass. The people buy sheep there from the Berbers and cut the meat into strips. This is carried by the people of Tuwāt to their country.

From that land we entered into a wilderness with no buildings in it and no water: it is three days' journey. Then we travelled after that fifteen days through a wilderness which has no buildings but there is water. We reached the place from which the road to Ghāt (which continues to Egypt) and the road to Tuwāt bifurcate. And there are there water-beds whose water flows over iron: when white cloths are washed in it, their colour becomes black. We travelled from there for ten [446]

73

days, and arrived at the country of the Hakkar [Ahoggar] who are a tribe of the Berbers and wear face-veils. There is no good in them. We were met by one of their big men and he held up the caravan until they gave him cloths and other things. Our arrival in their country was in the month of Ramaḍān; they do not attack nor intercept caravans in it. When their robbers find property in the roads in Ramaḍān they do not bother about it, and it is likewise for all the Berbers who are along this road. We journeyed a month in the land of Hakkar: it has a scarcity of plants and an abundance of stones, the road too is rough.

On the day of ʿId al-Fitr [the festival of fast-breaking] we reached the land of some Berbers who are people of the veil like these [i.e., the Hakkar]. They gave us news of our country and told us that the Awlād Khāraj and the banī Yaghmūr had risen up, and set themselves up in Tasābīt in Tuwāt. [447] The people of the caravan were afraid because of this. Then we reached Būdā which is one of the biggest villages of Tuwāt. Its soil consists of sand and saline swamp. Its dates are plentiful but not sweet; yet its people prefer them to the dates of Sijil-māsa. There is no cultivation there, no ghee, no olive oil. These things are brought to it from the land of the Maghrib. The food of its people is dates and locusts which are plentiful in their area. They preserve them as they store dates and feed on them. They go out to hunt locusts before sunrise when they cannot fly because of the cold.

We stayed at Būdā some days, then we travelled in a caravan and in the middle of Dhū' al-Qaʿda we arrived at the city of Sijilmāsa. I went out from it on the second of Dhū' al-Hijja [29 December A.D. 1353] during a period of fierce cold [448].

A lot of snow came down on the road. I have seen many rough roads and much snow in Būkhārā and Samarkand and in Khurāsān [in Persia] and in the land of the Turks, but I have never seen anything more difficult than the road of Umm Junaiba. We reached Dār al-Tamaᶜ on the night before ᶜId al-ᶜAḍhā. I stayed there the day of the festival, then I left and arrived at the capital Fās, the residence of our master, the commander of the faithful, may God support him! I kissed his noble hand and received the good fortune of seeing his blessed face. I stayed in the protection of his goodness after long travels, may God The Exalted recompense him for what he has given me of great kindness and overwhelming benefit! May He make his day everlasting, and give the Muslims the pleasure of his long life!

Here ends the travel narrative called 'A Gift to the Onlookers concerning the Curiosities of the Cities and the Wonders of the Journeys.' The completion of its dictation was on the third Dhū al-Ḥijja of the year [449] '56 [756 A.H., 9 December A.D. 1355). Praise be to God and peace be on his servants whom he has chosen!

Ibn Juzayy says, 'Here ends the abridgement from the dictation of the shaikh Abū ᶜAbd Allāh Muḥammad ibn Baṭṭūṭa (may God be gracious to him!). . . .'[80]

NOTES TO TRANSLATION

[1]The followers of Iman al Shāfiʿī constitute one of the four great rites or schools of law of the Sunni system. This remains the major school among Muslims in East Africa today. Its ways are characterized by a principled and traditionalist sunny common sense.

[2]Zeila and Mogadishu are in modern Somalia. Ibn Baṭṭūṭa and his editor have an admirable way of giving a careful 'fix' of some of the place names and difficult words he uses by spelling out the vowels. We have omitted this spelling and used the spelling he gives, except in the case of Mombasa, where we give it in full to show what such vocalization is like. Where clear modern equivalents to place names exist we have given them in brackets. *Rāfiḍi* were those who rejected the first three Caliphs. They were probably Shiʿa of some kind. They may have been Zaidī. Seyyid Aktar Rizvi of Dar-es-Salaam thinks they may have been Ithnāʿasharī (see Appendix II). Ibn Baṭṭūṭa was a staunch Sunni of the *Māliki* madhhab or school of law who had little sympathy for non-Sunnis.

[3]Richard Burton's *First Footsteps in East Africa*, edited by G. Waterfield and reissued, London, 1966, and the works of other Victorian travellers yield many interesting parallels and side-lights to ibn Baṭṭūṭa's narrative.

[4]*Faqīh* and *qāḍī* are difficult to translate. The first relates to the study of Muslim law. The title Ll.D. in its medieval sense of a doctor of canon and other law in some ways describes a *faqīh*, though it might rank him too high in the academic scale for often it became simply a title of honour for a respected scholar. The *qāḍī* is the official judge to do with Muslim law appointed by the ruler. On both see J. Schacht: *An Introduction to Islamic Law*, Oxford, 1964.

[5]*Sharīf*: a person who claims to be a descendant of the Prophet through Fāṭimā and ʿAlī. As such he can be given a place of honour in society and a share in alms. On the *sharīfs* see the Qur'ān VIII: 42, various *sharīf* family names in the *Encyclopaedia*

76

of Islam and R. B. Serjeant: *The Saiyids of Hadramawt*, London, 1957.

[6]This translates the Arabic as it stands. It may be a copyist's reading of the familiar *al Miṣrī* 'the Egyptian' for *al Muqrī*, the name of a family of jurists who were at the time established at this town. Ivan Hrbek, 'The Chronology of ibn Baṭṭūṭa's Travels', *Archiv Orientální* XXX, 1962, p. 412, based on Cerulli's article *Maḳdishū* in *Encyclopaedia of Islam*.

[7]*Mawlānā* is still used by Muslims in East Africa as an address of respect for people of royal status or for religious leaders.

[8]Betel leaves with areca nuts are still used in East Africa. *Pan-wallahs* offer various 'chews' costing from a few cents to five shillings. Presumably then, as now, direct Indian influence had its effect.

[9]At an East African *mawlidi* or celebration in honour of the birth of the Prophet, a *mrashi* is still used to sprinkle the people with perfumed water.

[10]*Wazīr* is another title with a range of meanings covering the spectrum from a Prime Minister to an officer in charge of some function in the royal kitchen. In ibn Baṭṭūṭa 'official' is as good a translation as any. He seems to confine the title *amir* to military officers of unspecified rank.

[11]'Ghee' is a Hindustani word which has come into English. It is a cooking fat made from milk. 'Large wooden dish': Arabic *ṣaḥfah*. Compare Kiswahili *chano*, a shallow wooden dish on which various foods can be set forth. The word translated 'fish' a little lower down is the same word used in the Qur'ān to describe the great fish which swallowed Jonah. H. F. Janssens in his *Ibn Batouta*, Brussels, 1948, commends Gibb's remark that our author was a 'geographer despite himself.'His own remark that this work is 'un atlas gastronomique de l'Orient' (p. 89) as well as his lively account of the life and times of the author deserves commendation. He regrets that the great traveller's religion precluded his enjoyment of the local wines.

[12]Mrs. Sophia Hamdun remarks that much of this description

of food would apply to hospitality on the East Coast to this day. She adds that ibn Baṭṭūṭa as a mere man may have mistaken the coconut milk used in cooking the banana for fresh milk. Regarding mangoes, the usual Arabic word today is *manaj*—to which 'mango' would appear to be related, though it is said the word came into European languages from Tamil. His word *ᶜanbah* and its collective *ᶜanbūn* (compare *tamar, tamrūn*: dates) are related to Kiswahili *-embe* and both may have some connection with the antecedent of the Hindi *anb*, Urdu *āmb*. The word translated 'chillies' is *fulfil*, compare Kiswahili *pilipili*.

13'The royal enclosure': after Muᶜāwiyya escaped the attack in the mosque to which ᶜAlī succumbed, Muslim monarchs sometimes provided themselves with an enclosure to protect them at prayer.

14It would be natural if some corruption crept into the text of descriptions of exotic clothes and foods. Dr. Humphrey Fisher has here, and in other places, corrected our text and we have adopted his suggestions. His note here reads as follows: 'Gibb says "with fine robes of Egyptian stuffs with their appendages (?) underneath it," and suggests a copyist's error distorting an original *mutarrazāt*, "embroideries." The Beirut (1960) edition says *tarūhāt* which are something thrown on the shoulders, whence my suggested word "loose".' The panoply of kingship is most interesting. One is reminded of an Ashanti *durbar* when the kings walked with dignity beneath state umbrellas. In Ghana the four canopies were superimposed on the same carrying handle and one bird presided over all. It is possible that the umbrella came to African kings from the Hindu god-kings. Some commentary on African sacral ruler-cult is also given in the section on the visit to Malli.

15The difference between the cases decided by the *qāḍī* and those decided by the group may have been the difference between the law of the *sharīᶜa* which was known to the *qāḍī* as an expert who had to set out what the law said, and traditional law where a group of old men who knew many cases and precedents would give a verdict on behalf of customary law.

[16]*Bilād as-sawāhil*: our author's use would indicate that he thought of it as a land south from Mombasa, including the coasts of what we would now call northern Tanzania and perhaps the islands. Having sailed past Lamu, Malindi and Gedi out at sea, ibn Baṭṭūṭa first touched the lands we would associate with the word 'Swahili' at Mombasa. Kilwa would be towards their southern side, but the Islands of the Moon (Comoro) were perhaps excluded. On the use of the expression 'the coast lands' we may compare the use of *mrima* in Mombasa: people going over the causeway refer to the mainland as *mrima*. The student will find G. S. P. Freeman-Grenville's *The East African Coast, Select Documents*, Oxford, 1962, and *The Medieval History of the Coast of Tanganyika*, London, 1962, well worth consulting. The root *z-n-j* remains a mystery. As used here, it seems to indicate the black people of the East African coast and islands. H. O. Hunwick's 'The term *zanj* and its derivatives in a West African chronicle' in D. Dalby, ed., *Language and History in Africa*, 1970, pp. 102-108, is not relevant to the East African meaning. *Zunūj*, the form used here, is of course a plural and refers to the people. On 'the land of Zinj or Zanj' compare *bilād as-sūdān*. We had considered using *Zinj* or *Zanj* but finally decided to keep the plural. *Kulwa*-'Kilwa' is more usual. His Manbasaᶜ is more correct than 'Mombasa.'

[17]Mombasa is an island close to the mainland. Ibn Baṭṭūṭa says it has no *barr*—hinterland, meaning no mainland dependencies. Today going up to the hinterland (in Kiswahili *bara*) in Mombasa can include almost anywhere in Kenya and Uganda. The great traveller was there only a short time. It is indeed unlikely that there was no cultivation there, probably he means the cultivation of normal cereals. The banana had, as he states, already reached the Sawaḥil (from Indonesia perhaps via Madagascar). It is probable that he is mistaken over the mosques being made of wood. It seems likely that the mosques were of stone. Perhaps he used some rare word for coral which scribes changed to a more familiar word, or the mosques had wooden facings. Most probably his memory deceived him. His description of certain ways of carrying out the ablutions at Mombasa is most

accurate. The *kata*, a ladle made out of half a coconut or an empty jam can with a handle stuck through it, is still used. Modern religious scholars coming from Mombasa say there is more footwear there today, but add modestly that the high standards of integrity and religion have inevitably wilted a little before an influx of foreigners.

[18]*Jammūn*: *Hobson-Jobson*, that magnificent dictionary of the Anglo-Indian language edited by Yule and Burnell, has recently been reissued and enables us to recognize this as *eugenia jambolana*. Various things sweet and plum-like seem to be able to carry the name. Cf. also Platt's *Dictionary of Urdu and Classical Hindi s.v. janbu*, the rose-apple.

[19]Kilwa has been extensively excavated. Neville Chittick's report in *Azania* I, 1966, pp. 1-36, gives an account of the work and a full bibliography. Even in ruins it is an impressive site on its island. When ibn Baṭṭūṭa visited it it must indeed have been one of the fairest towns in tropical Africa or indeed the world. It would seem it depended for its prosperity on the slave and ivory trade converging on it from the Rufiji and Ruvuma routes in the direction of Lake Malawi as well as on its position as a staging post in the gold trade through Sofala with *regnum Monomotapiae* and the gold producing areas in the Sofala hinterland. The Portuguese sacked the city in 1507 and broke the links in the north-south gold trade. Various wild tribes broke down the inland trade. Kilwa has never recovered, not even in its late Arab form of Kilwa Kivinje or the colonial Kilwa Masoko. H. A. R. Gibb, *The Travels of Ibn Baṭṭūṭa*, Hakluyt Series, vol. II, Cambridge, 1962, (abbreviated hereafter as Hakluyt II) p. 380, note 61, takes it Yūfī is Nupe and that ibn Baṭṭūṭa has confused the gold dust of the Niger with the mined gold of Sofala. It is possible that ibn Baṭṭūṭa or, more likely, his editor, did confuse things in this way. Possibly we shall discover that there was inland from Sofala a source of gold with a name like Yūfī. We shall meet Yūfī again in the West African section.

[20]Defrémery and Sanguinetti's *Variantes et Notes* at page 455 give a number of variants for j-*n*-d. Gibb (Hakluyt II, p. 380,

note 59) accepts j-*n-w* and connects it with the word which came into European languages as 'Guinea,' roughly the non-Muslim forest and coastal belt of West Africa. We prefer to leave it unidentified.

[21]*Kunya*: this is the Arabic term for an additional name given to someone—'son of', 'father of'. It can be extended to physical features 'father of the forked beard' or to features of character, as in this case. Both the writers on meeting this one, 'father of grants', thought of certain officials of the Rockefeller Foundation who had enabled us as scholars of religion to imitate ibn Baṭṭūṭa in a small way.

[22]Gibb (Hakluyt II, p. 382, note 67) reckons ibn Baṭṭūṭa probably left Kilwa with the southwest monsoon about the end of March. According to old East African dhow travellers, he would take four weeks to reach Arabia or a little more for India.

[23]For general background reading to this section of the *Travels* there is an extensive number of books. The relevant part of Gibb's Hakluyt series has not appeared, but see his selections in Broadway Travellers series published in 1929 and reprinted a number of times. Everyone who teaches Medieval Civilizations longs to have this available in paperback. We refer to it as *Selections*. We would recommend especially E. W. Bovill's *Caravans of the Old Sahara* which was re-written and re-issued in 1958 as *The Golden Trade of the Moors*. W. D. Cooley's *The Negroland of the Arabs*, London, 1841, reprinted 1966, does not help the non-expert much. C. Monteil, *Les empires du Mali*, Paris, 1929, reprinted 1968; D. T. Niane, *Recherches sur l'empire du Mali au moyen âge*, Conakry, 1962, and R. Mauny, V. Monteil, A. Djenidi, S. Robert, J. Devisse, *Extraits tires des voyages d'Ibn Baṭṭūṭa*, Dakar, 1966 (abbreviated as Mauny *et al. Extraits*), are most helpful. Nehemia Levtzion's writing is also most relevant —the article in the *Journal of African History* which we cite below; 'The Early States of the Western Sudan to 1500' which appears as a chapter in J. F. A. Ajayi and M. Crowder's *History of West Africa*, London, 1971, as well as his important book

Ancient Ghana and Mali, London, 1973, and a paper on 'The differential impact of Islam among the Soninke and Manding' given at the important conference on Manding Studies which was held at the London School of Oriental and African Studies in the summer of 1972. A number of the other papers presented have bearing on our subject and have generously been made available in mimeographed form. No doubt they will be published in due course. We also acknowledge the courtesy of the Centre for West African Studies at Birmingham, England, for allowing us to see W. Rajkowski and J. F. P. Hopkins, *Arabic Material Relating to the Western Sudan*, which is to be published soon.

[24]The Massūfa were one of the major tribes of Berber nomads who inhabited the Sahara. *Anli* is a name of Berber origin for a kind of small-grained millet which was probably independently domesticated in West Africa. The botanical name is *pennisetum typhoideum*. For botanical information see J. M. Dalziel, *The Useful Plants of West Tropical Africa*, London, 1937. His indices of vernacular terms, scientific and common names makes his book most useful. A. P. Murdock, *Africa, Its Peoples and their Culture History*, New York, 1959, has a lot of information on the history of plants but only carries an index of tribal names.

[25]*Mithqāl*: a measure of weight, in this case, for weight in gold. It is difficult to determine an equivalence. M. G. C. Miles (*The Coinage of the Umayyads of Spain*, two volumes, New York, 1950) and Lévi-Provencal (*Histoire de l'espagne musulmane*, vol. III, Paris, 1953) give various opinions, but on the whole it looks as if in our author's time in the west the *mithqāl* weighed about 4.6 to 4.8 grammes. Mauny *et al.*, *Extraits*, p. 36, value it at 39.295 French francs of 1964. The *qinṭar* mentioned just further on was in Egypt the equivalent of 44.93 kilogrammes and in Tunisia to 53.9. (Compare French *quintal* and Latin *centenarius*). See also Walter Hinz, *Islamische Masse und Gewichte*, Leiden, 1955.

[26]Mauny *et al.*, *Extraits*, p. 37, say this distance was about 250 kilometres.

[27]Tāsarahlā is located by Mauny *et al.*, *Extraits*, p. 38 and map

on p. 32, as 250 km. due south of Taghāzā and 480 km. north northeast from Īwālātan. *Takshīf*: literally 'the discovery,' hence 'the uncoverer' or 'scout'.

[28]The *Farba* as representing the king would partake in part of his sacral monarchy. He was sitting perhaps under some kind of arched lintel and like many West African monarchs spoke through a 'spokesman' or herald (cf. the Ghanaian *okyeame* who is used even when the king speaks to his own people). It was not insolence but normal local good manners. Ibn Baṭṭūta was, alas, not the last white man to regret his arrival; luckily Africans overlook such over-hasty feelings based on ignorance, and most often the worst culprits among the strangers come to look back on their visit with appreciation.

[29]Manshā Jū is probably *mansā dyon*, meaning 'servant of the king.' It is indeed surprising that a seasoned traveller such as our author did not grasp the symbolism of a fellowship meal where the staple food together with milk and honey were served. Apart from the offering of the basic and the pleasantest food, it signified that no black arts would be used against one and reciprocally it meant the recipient would behave loyally. Probably ibn Baṭṭūta's age and eminence were weighing him down and he expected special treatment.

[30]Many sub-Saharan African tribes are matrilineal; as the Akan proverb says, 'Everybody knows who a person's mother is.' It is a matter of the blood being provided by the mother. To a child, the mother's brother is the most important male in the group. This has led to a great deal of friction where this kind of society has met Islam (and indeed, western society). Islam, on the whole, has been extremely tolerant and patient, but in the end the change-over has come. It is still possible to trace it in process amongst living informants, for instance among the Yao of south-west Tanzania. African society has been even more tenacious in refusing to bring its women-folk into a position of apparent bashful withdrawal, and African Muslims may be heard to say this is not essential to Islam as a religion, but is part of the cultural vessel.

³¹On the journey between Walata and Malli see the paper read at the London Manding Conference of 1972 by Claude Meillassoux. This scholar, who appears to be familiar with the actual topography, presents a number of valuable alternatives as well as probable sites, a detailed bibliography, and a sketch map. See also his article in *The Journal of African History*, vol. XIII, 3, 1972, pp. 389-395.

³²This is a note by ibn Juzayy, ibn Baṭṭūṭa's editor, who came from Spain. Our traveller is obviously speaking of that magnificent feature of parts of the African landscape, the baobab. See Dalziel, *Useful Plants*, p. 112f. Ibn Baṭṭūṭa's picture of travel through West Africa remains strangely true to this day despite the coming of the 'mammy wagon', the motor lorry, which almost more than any other material thing has transformed West Africa. One can see the market women with their pounded foods, their calabashes and almost read the counterpart of the notice 'carved calabash is here'.

³³Said Hamdun says that his people at Mombasa take the baobab fruit and pound it into a kind of flour. This fruit looks rather like a cucumber or outsize sausage.

³⁴*Gharti*: soninké: *kharite*, shea butter. The tree is to be seen dotted about in the West African savannah, somehow surviving the bush-fires and the goats. The women collect the nuts, prepare and sell the oil. A few thousand of them in a market is a sight never to be forgotten. With ibn Baṭṭūṭa's remarks we may compare Dalziel's (p. 353) 'if clarified, native-prepared shea butter can be used quite acceptably for European cooking'. To the uses ibn Baṭṭūṭa gives, add 'to pomade the hair and to make a soap'.

³⁵*Tāsirghant*: a word of Berber derivation; the root of *telephium imperati* which grows in the Maghrib, and is used in perfumery. Though some of the forms of maize, some beans, root-crops, ground-nuts, etc., so prominent in West Africa today are descended from crops introduced from the Americas, West Africa carried out her own agricultural revolution in prehistoric times and there were indigenous counterparts and pre-

decessors to most of the immigrant varieties. *Kuskus (couscous)* is still well known in North Africa. It is a wheat or groats made into a paste and cooked. Meat or vegetables are served with it. *Nabaq* is a Christ's thorn (*ziziyphus spinachristi*) whose fruit (called in English 'lotus') can be dried and made into a flour. *Fonio* is a cereal like semolina. The problem over the rice is a puzzle unless it was a native variety with some poison in its skin which had to be cooked a very long time, or perhaps the danger feared was beri-beri. A little further on ibn Baṭṭūṭa tells how he ate a kind of *qalqās*—colocasia, coco-yam, or similar edible root—which almost killed him. Probably it had not been cooked long enough.

[36]The Khārijites were those early Muslims who separated themselves from those who submitted divine matters to human arbitration. The ruling class in the ͨUmānī sultanate of Zanzibar were Ibāḍi. Ivor Wilkes says the Ṣaghanaghū are 'a specialized "clerical" lineage existing in symbiotic relationship with the Dyula groups, whose association, historically, has been with commerce. They are widely spread in West Africa, particularly in the Ivory Coast and western Upper Volta.' (*Research Bulletin of the Centre of Arabic Documentation* II, 2, Ibadan, 1966, pp. 11f.)

[37]*Māliki* refers to the Sunni school of law which remains dominant in West Africa. Both ibn Baṭṭūṭa and his editor belonged to it. *Tūrī* is a patronymic still used in West Africa for a number of 'marabutic' lineages. In the beginning it may have referred to their sacral status or origin but today it is very loosely employed.

[38]Zāgha is probably Diagha at the south-west edge of the Masina flood-plain. The other places named, where no equivalent is given to them below in brackets, are not directly identifiable. Where a reasonable guess at their location is possible, they are named on the map.

[39]Ibn Baṭṭūṭa takes it that the great river of West Africa is the Nile and that it continued eastward from where he last saw it in West Africa to the highest point where he had seen the Nile; that is, in Upper Egypt. It was a pardonable mistake based on what he had seen with his own eyes, what was reported to him,

and the natural human desire to accept the most simple hypo-
thesis to explain observed phenomena. His remarks on religion
in Nubia are particularly interesting, for they indicate the sur-
vival of Christianity, though the monarch of Dongola, their
great stronghold, had become Muslim. Recent excavations
before the flooding caused by the Aswan Dam will no doubt
add much to our knowledge. The periodical *Kush* has since 1963
carried most fascinating reports and serves as a guide to the
mass of other literature appearing. *Al-malik al-nāṣir* is probably
the *mamlūk* sultan of Egypt, Muḥammad, known as the victori-
ous rule, who ruled Egypt thrice, 1293-4, 1298-1308 and 1309-
40.

[40]The River Ṣanṣara: Mauny *et al.*, (*Extraits*, p. 49f.) and M.
Delafosse ('Le Gana et Mali et l'emplacement de leurs capitales',
Bulletin du comite d'etudes historiques et scientifique de l'A.O.F., 1924,
pp. 528f.) take it that this is probably the River Sankarani which
runs into the Niger 80 kilometres southwest of Bamako. They
add that the word *Mali* is of *soninke* origin and signifies 'the
capital'. A summary of the debate will be found in J. O.
Hunwick's paper 'The Mid-Fourteenth Century Capital of
Mali' read at the Manding Conference of 1972. He concludes
that it is not possible yet to pinpoint the location accurately but
'attention should be concentrated on the left bank of the Niger,
downstream from Bamako to about as far as Niamina'. See also
his article in *The Journal of African History* XIV, 2, 1973, pp.
195-208.

[41]On the various details mentioned by our author in connection
with dynastic politics in Malli see Nawal Bell's paper presented
to the Manding Conference on 'The Age of Mansā Mūsa of
Mali: Problems in Succession and Chronology', and N. Levtzion: 'The thirteenth and fourteenth century kings of Mali',
Journal of African History IV, 3, 1961, pp. 341-353. Levtzion
shows by studying other sources, especially ibn Khaldūn, that
our author was somewhat confused about collateral branches of
the royal family and the intrigues going on; for instance, the
rivalry between the house of Mansā Mūsa and the house of his

brother Mansā Sulaimān. The genealogical table given by Levtzion makes the matter clear. For our purposes here it is probably sufficient to mention the following points:

(1) The Sāriq-Djāta whom our author says was converted to Islam and was Mansā Mūsa's grandfather is to be identified with the first Mārī-Djāta who was a *brother* of Mūsa's grandfather. Musa's line was collateral to this Mārī-Djāta's line.

(2) After Mūsa's (1312-37) death his successor Mansā Maghā ruled for only a few years before the power was taken over by Mūsa's brother Sulaimān. Sulaimān died in 1360 and before long his successor was deposed by Mūsa's line.

(3) Ibn Baṭṭūṭa says the Qāsā appealed to Djātal. Levtzion states that Sulaimān succeeded in thwarting this plot in 1352 or 1353, but seven years later his successor was deposed by another Mārī-Djāta (1360-73) who belonged to Mūsa's line and may be identified with our author's 'Djātal'.

Most people familiar with medieval history and the complications of merging matriarchal systems, let alone rotating succession, would give ibn Baṭṭūṭa high marks for his performance under such a test, especially when competing with an historical genius such as ibn Khaldūn whose findings may yet be given pause when oral tradition has been properly collated.

42The deceased was the Marinid sultan of Fez who reigned till 1351. Muslim honorifics to most westerners are quaint and redolent of the East of romance. East African Muslims like to know their proper use and often interject them most correctly into addresses and recitations as a kind of antiphonal response. Here is the Hamdun concise guide to some of them:

(1) 'May God be pleased with him,' after the name of a person to be honoured religiously.

(2) 'The Exalted', 'the Most High', after the name of God.

(3) 'May God grant him blessing and peace,' (in printing abbreviated to S.A.W. on the basis of the Arabic initial letters) after the name of the Prophet Muhammad.

(4) 'Upon him, peace,' after the name of prophets other than Muhammad.

(5) 'May God have mercy on him,' after the name of someone

87

dead. Where living and dead are prayed for together, the prayer is for forgiveness for the dead and for the living, long life. 'Reading stools': *al-raba'āt* may rather be boxes or biers used for a kind of memorial 'funeral'.

[43]There are various ceremonies including alms-giving connected with the 27th, *lailat al-qadr*, the night of power when angels descend with blessing. The local use on which ibn Baṭṭūṭa is commenting is that there they call it *zakāt*, though normally that applies to the legal alms proper. Compare the northern Nigerian use of *ṣalla* (*salāt*) for a particular public festival prayer when its regular use is for the prescribed daily prayers.

[44]*Zardkhāna*: Said Hamdun remarked 'this word has a Persian air', if so, it may have to do with yellow embroidered robes. It may be a kind of silk embroidered with the forms of animals.

[45]'Pages': this word is used to indicate boys and young men at an African court. For instance at Kabaka Muteesa's court these lads from all over Buganda, not necessarily of royal or aristocratic blood, learnt the business of government and afterwards went out as chiefs and royal officials.

[46]In various parts of Africa the king sits on a platform made of earth which is raised a few feet above the surrounds but is large enough to allow a certain number of people to stand on it around the main person. Probably the *banbi* was such a platform which could perhaps mean also 'seat of government'. The word is probably related to the Mandinke *bembe*, bench, platform.

[47]*Shaṭr*: this is translated 'umbrella' though it is in Arabic an unusual word. Perhaps it is related to the Indian word which appears in Gujerati as *chtri*, the umbrella being an ancient emblem of kingship in India. Silken umbrellas topped by emblems such as birds are still carried over Akan kings in Ghana.

[48]*Muṭanfas*: it is difficult to say exactly what kind of cloth this was. By 'Roman' an Arab writer could mean 'Byzantine' or use it to mean very much what Africans today mean by the word 'European'. There was a good amount of trade between the

lands subject to Constantinople, various parts of Italy and the islamic world in the fourteenth century.

[49]*Qanābir*: probably represents *ganābir* (singular *ganbri*) which are like the two-stringed guitars still used in North Africa. Farmer's *History of Arabian Music*, London, 1929, reprinted in 1967, mentions instruments of this kind, such as the *qītāra* used in al-Andalus.

[50]The account of kingship customs is strongly reminiscent of the Byzantine ceremonial connected with the king in his *consistorium*, the ceremony of *proskynēsis* and the victory cult. (See N. Q. King: *There's Such Divinity Doth Hedge a King*, London, 1960.) This is not necessarily to imply that African kingship copied the Byzantine, though the Nubian kingdoms could have received and transmitted such influences. Similar ceremonies could be witnessed in Uganda at Mmengo, Hoima and Mbarara till 1966. As Professor S. H. Hooke admitted in his eighty-sixth year, 'spontaneous generation seems a simpler solution than diffusion'. In any case, one has to be on one's guard against saying pure African traditional kingship was autocratic. In certain cases as a result of disintegration or recent manoeuvres by the monarch it could become tyrannous. With regard to the 'dusting', this is found quite often in East African circumcision rituals as a means of warding off misfortune at a time of exposure or when the numinous is present in uncovered and raw form. Though abject ruler-cult obtruded itself in certain islamic kingdoms, Islam tends to deprecate such customs. It is said that it was a certain Muslim (Arab or Swahili) who was the first to dare to rebuke a Kabaka for executing his subjects, pointing out that he and they were subjects of Allah.

Ibn Baṭṭūṭa at another place (IV 302f.—while describing customs in China) mentions that some of the people of the land of the blacks, when their king dies, dig a deep tomb and bury with him some of the king's friends, slaves, the children of noblemen, and vessels full of food. They break the arms and the legs of the victims. One of the Massūfa who was living among the people of the land of Kūbar (Gobir) had difficulty in saving his son from being buried alive with the sultan who had recently died. Archaeology has shown this was a custom carried on without any possibility of cultural diffusion in many different parts of the world.

[51]The description of the shape of festival ritual in Islamic Africa in the fourteenth century may prove to be of as great interest to comparative liturgiologists as Saint Luke's synagogue service at Nazareth or Saint Ambrose's basilican service when he was able to exhort and rebuke the emperor.

[52]*Ṭailasān*: the word is still used at Mombasa to indicate the white headgear of the prayer leader or Friday preacher. In West Africa it can indicate the light cotton head and shoulder covering worn by the learned among the Muslims.

[53]Arabic: *yūhallilūn wa yukabbirūn*.

[54]In 1965 a manuscript notebook of the late Shaikh Sekyim-wanyi, who is reputed to have been the first *muganda* to make the pilgrimage, was brought to Makerere. It contained sermon notes in Arabic for use at the great Festivals and the subjects covered were much the same as those mentioned by ibn Baṭṭūṭa. Probably they are just about the same everywhere in the Islamic world.

[55]Just as there are festal days differentiated from the ferial and associated with the octaves of certain great Christian festivals, so there are special days associated with the great Islamic festivals. These are usually two days after the feast itself, which with the day itself make a triad.

[56]Ingenious African historians in search of pre-colonial datings use such data as the spread of the banana and the xylophone. It is probable that an instrument as complicated as this would be introduced or invented in one place and then spread by diffusion. Circumcision of adolescents or deformation of ox horns could probably be discovered spontaneously in many places.

[57]These are the famous Manding *griots* or bards, men of the reciter class. The custom of 'poets' and 'singers' standing before

90

kings to recite the deeds of the past and the king's own deeds, is ancient and widespread in Africa. In a pre-literate society, till Muslim scribes began to write down these things, they were the 'memories' and historians of the community. Their task was no laughing matter for in many places if they stumbled in the recitation or made a mistake, they paid for it with their lives. They also had the fearful privilege of bringing aberrations from the past to the attention of the king and by their cult of victory ensuring victory. They often wore costumes, partly to put on a *persona* to show they did not speak as individuals in their own right, but more because spirits came and dwelt in them. It is doubtful whether the hobby horse in English May-day ceremonial was considered ridiculous in the days when morris dancing was not a mere revival.

The word translated 'a bird' is *al-shaqshāq*, which probably represents *al-shaqrāq*, a bird of speckled green, red and white found around Mecca (Al Fairūzabādī: *al-Qāmūs al Muhīt*). Which African bird is intended, one cannot be sure.

[58]This account reminds one of certain forms of Semitic prophecy and divination (see Guillaume's book of that title, London, 1938). The pious man beholds the locusts, in number, they are *too great* (Ar. *kathīr*), this causes a voice to impinge upon his consciousness to say that they come to punish the *too great* (*yakthuru*) wrong in the land. Compare Amos who sees the *awake* tree and hears a voice saying God is *awake*: and locusts in the Hebrew Bible and the Qur'ān as punishers of wrong.

[59]For a Muslim of ibn Baṭṭūṭa's type, this would be most unusual. *Kāsa* in Mandinke indicates the queen or first wife of the ruler. The 'woman-king' is often important in African kingship. She was a sovereign in her own right. Often she was not in fact the king's spouse but a female monarch chosen from the princesses of the blood royal. We may be in this narrative witnessing the sultan's attempt to replace the African type of queen by the consort-type of queen, a person who owed her position to her husband.

[60]*Jaṭal* probably represents the Mandinka *dyata*, 'lion', a fairly

common name, but see the note above on dynastic politics in Malli.

⁶¹Mansā Mūsa brought Abū Ishāq, who came from Grenada, back with him from Mecca. Ibn Baṭṭūṭa was shortly to visit the latter's grave at Timbuktu. At the London Manding Conference of 1972, J. O. Hunwick presented a paper about him entitled 'An Andalusian in Mali'.

⁶²Cf. Qur'ān VI: 161, 'The man that does good shall receive tenfold.'

⁶³A tradition tells us to encourage a child to pray at seven and beat him at ten if he does not.

⁶⁴Ibn Baṭṭūṭa was going northeastwards towards Timbuktu along the great bend of the river system. He seems to have met two of Africa's great enemies and guardians, the tsetse fly (which made horses dear) and the mosquito (which kept out white men). The latter bite more at night than in the day so some other insect may be intended. On the method of hippo-potamus hunting which he mentions, see J. P. Rouch: *Les Songhay*, Paris, 1954, pp. 21-22. The method was apparently still in use on parts of the Niger Bend till prohibited by the colonial authorities.

⁶⁵This famous pilgrimage took place in 1324 and 1325.

⁶⁶It is amazing how ingenuous and gullible this experienced traveller can be: he passes on these excellent stories to prove white men are both immature and dishonest, both told with obvious gusto and laughter by his sophisticated African in-formant. Later, when some people make a meal of his camel, they tell him it had died, he rushes out to find they have already eaten it. His only emotion is disgust at their eating a dead animal.

⁶⁷This is Chapter XXXVI of the Qur'ān and is still read daily by many Muslims especially in commemoration of a dead friend or relative or as a *memento mori* for themselves. It is perhaps a sign that our author realized that he was getting old and his

death was drawing near. We may compare the use of Psalm XXIII or John XIV by some Christians.

⁶⁸Gibb's *Selections* renders this as 'Little Saucepan'.

⁶⁹'The birthday of the Prophet': the *maulid* is very popular in East Africa today. If the celebration of the birthday was brought into *mamlūk* Egypt by analogy with Christmas, this mention of it illustrates how closely the land of the blacks was linked to Egypt in matters Islamic.

⁷⁰It is a comment on the distribution of books in the medieval Islamic world to find a theological work written in Baghdad about a century and a half earlier being read by a West African. The avidity with which ibn Baṭṭūṭa takes it up evokes the sympathy of any who have to travel when they want to study. Ibn al-Jawzī is described as a Ḥanbalite who died in 597/1200. The book was a compilation of Qur'ānic knowledge and tradition.

⁷¹In West Africa one is still assured by a number of the Scots medical men who serve there that the water is dangerous. It seems that statistics prove more die there by drinking the water than by whisky.

⁷²'Growing boy': the Arabic literally means 'five spans high', i.e., not fully grown.

⁷³'Cowries': these shells used to be used as currency in various parts of Africa. Today they are used in ritual ornaments, the Comparative Religions man's usual imaginative explanation being that they are fertility symbols. The shells themselves are supposed to have come from the Indian Ocean, though how in antiquity they reached West Africa from there is a puzzle. Ibn Baṭṭūṭa mentions them while in the Maldives [IV 121]. He remarks that at Malli and Jūjū (Gao) they were sold at a thousand, one hundred and fifty for a gold dinar. See also Marion Johnson, 'The cowrie currencies of West Africa', *Journal of African History*, vol. XI, 1970, pp. 17-49, 331-353.

ᶜinānī: whether this indicates a type of pumpkin or a place which grows them, it has not been possible to establish.

[74]This is as graceful and pleasing a compliment as any host could hope to earn.

[75]The *mudd* is a variable cubic measure. Taking the *shenbul* as our unit, the *mudd* was about one-sixth of it; that is, perhaps it was equivalent to eighteen litres. (*Shenbul* may be related to the word 'bushel' and *mudd* to the Latin *modius*.) The estimates of various scholars consulted varies from 0.75 litres to 46.6.

[76]Early in a sojourn in West Africa a good steward will explain to the tenderfoot: 'Scorpion injection go killee pickin'; trouble man, pain pass all.'

[77]As Evelyn King remarked: 'Nowadays one has to offer them marriage.'

[78]A number of monarchs in north-eastern Nigeria have retained this custom of speaking from behind curtains down to modern times. It is one of the traits of divine kingship picked out for instance in Tor Istram: *The King of Ganda*, Stockholm, 1944. In connection with the recruitment of slaves, one of the writers was amazed to discover at Salaga in North Ghana old men who had witnessed the creation of eunuchs for service in the Turkish imperial service.

[79]No doubt the poor souls were by now clad in Mother Hubbards from their ankles to their chins using cloth manufactured by the counterpart of the Manchester cotton mills.

[80]This is the full title according to the flowery custom of the day; but the work is more familiarly known as the *Rihla*, which may be rendered, 'the travel-narrative', or 'travels'. Ibn Juzayy's remark on ibn Baṭṭūṭa, 'May God be gracious to him', indicates that the latter was still alive when he wrote his conclusion to the work.

APPENDIX I

Ibn Baṭṭūṭa was a young man when he made his first visit to black Africa. In 726 A.H./A.D. 1326, he was in Egypt and wanted to go to Mecca. He went up the Nile to Luxor in southern Egypt, across the Nile at Adfū and thence across the desert for fifteen days to the town of ʿAidhāb on the African side of the Red Sea. He found that the people were Bujā (Beja), black in colour, wearing yellow robes with head-ties about a finger's width wide. They did not permit their daughters to inherit. The town belonged two-thirds to their king and one-third to the king of Egypt. At that town he visited a mosque rich in *baraka* and a venerable shaikh who claimed to be a son of a Moroccan king. He discovered that the mamlūk soldiers from Egypt had been defeated by the local sultan who had sunk the shipping. The journey across the Red Sea to Jeddah was impossible, so ibn Baṭṭūṭa had to sell his provisions and return to Cairo the same way he had come. The Nile was in flood so this part of the journey only took eight days. He hurried on to Syria and continued his travels. [I 109-111].

A few years later (730 A.H./A.D. 1329-1330) ibn Baṭṭūṭa set out from Judda (Jeddah) and sailed for two days. The weather then became rough and they were blown to an anchorage off the African coast called Ra's Dawā'ir which is between ʿAidhāb and the island of Sawākin. There he found a shelter of reeds made on the model of a mosque and ostrich shells full of water.

There was also a tide-race in which the people caught great fish just by putting in a cloth and holding it at both ends. Once again he met the Bujā (Beja) and travelled with them over a plain full of deer. They came upon an Arab encampment belonging to the Awlād Kāhil who have mixed with the Bujā. Then they went on to the island of Sawākin. Water had to be brought to it but it exported milk-products and some coarse grain to Mecca. The sultan of Sawākin was closely connected to the *amīrs* of Mecca through his father, but the island came to him through his mother's Bujā relations. [II 160-163]

Fom Sawākin, ibn Baṭṭūṭa went to Al-Yaman and found his way to ʿAdan (Aden).

Two years later, ibn Baṭṭūṭa again visited this coast on his way from Mecca to India. He had tried to get a ship going directly from Jedda but when he failed to do so, he crossed over to the African side of the Red Sea, making for ʿAidhāb. Unfortunately, he was driven by the wind to Ra's Dawā'ir and had to go overland nine days across very dry country before he reached ʿAidhāb. The Bujā controlled the area, although there were also some Arabs there. An Arab youth who was a slave to the Bujā said that he had lived on camel's milk for a year. Ibn Baṭṭūṭa was able to hire camels and make his way on to the Nile and travel to Cairo [II 251-254].

From there he went to India by way of Asia Minor and southern Russia. He mentions without details that he passed ʿAidhāb again in the reverse direction on his way to Mecca in 1348 after he had visited China [IV 324]. After this he returned home, visited Spain, and then set out on his last great journey to Malli, which is for him *the* land of the blacks.

APPENDIX II

RUINS OF A SULTAN'S PALACE AT AN EAST AFRICAN COASTAL CITY STATE
(14TH CENTURY)

A NOTE ON SHĪꜥA CONNECTIONS WITH THE EARLY HISTORY OF EAST AFRICA[1]
By Seyyid Said Akhtar Rizvi

Oral traditions in the Lamu, Zanzibar and Mombasa areas yield evidence that some of the early Muslim travellers and settlers coming from Arabia and the Persian Gulf down the East African coast had Shīꜥa connections. By the time ibn Baṭṭūṭa came he found that in places like Mogadishu, Mombasa, and Kilwa the Shāfiꜥī Sunnis were long established and he gives little hint that there had been Shīꜥa influence. Presumably a change-over had taken place some long time before he visited. This could easily happen, either by predominance of numbers, change of dynasty, or intermarriage. The attrition of numbers undergone in recent years by the Ibāḍī followers of the sultans of Zanzibar, many of whose descendants have conformed to Sunni practice, may be comparable.

Though the local oral tradition about early Shīꜥa influence is so strong, it is difficult to pin it down in detail. It is easy also to pepper it full of holes with the grape-shot of historical criticism, but the general fact that Shīꜥa groups came early to this coast can be taken as proven. The systematic collection and sifting of oral material has still to be done and archaeology is rendering increasing service.

In looking through the written material again, it becomes

clear that there is a fair amount of apparently tangential material which may be useful. Let us give two examples. (1) The classical Swahili literature which is becoming available in increasing quantity should help us. For instance, *Utenzi wa Seyyidna Huseni Bin Ali* ('The poem of our Lord Husein the son of Ali') is by Shaikh Hemed Abdullah el-Buhry dating from the nineteenth century but is probably based on an earlier work.[2] The poet narrates that when Muhammad al-Hanafiyya heard the news of the martyrdom of Imam Husein, he rode alone towards Kufa. On his way he looked ahead, and he saw a rock standing in front of him. He told his horse to turn aside on the right and then on the left, but there was no way through. So he turned back and he was astonished because there was no way back. He was hemmed in by rocks. Then he heard a voice from heaven telling him that he would remain there till before the end of the world when he would come out and take vengeance for Imām Husein. 'Then the rocks closed in on his right and on his left and the Lord placed him inside in a secret place, and his name is Mahdi. He is the Mahdi who is to come and of whom you all have heard.'

This legend is typical Kaisānīyya material. This sect withered away in the first half of the eighth century. The story narrated in this *utenzi* may have reached the East African coast before or about the middle of the eighth century. Not only the historical facts but even the names and relationships of the famous personalities of the tragedy of Karbala have been twisted and distorted to a great extent, suggesting a very long gap between the original storytelling and its being written down into the form in which we meet it.

102

(2) The surviving parts of the Kilwa Chronicle have been known to historians for some time, but insufficient attention has been paid to one aspect of the Arabic Preface.[3] In it (ms. page 3, bottom three lines, page 4, top line) the writer praises 'Reason and its requirements, because it is only by Reason that things can be known, and on it alone is the foundation of the commandments of God, which were brought by the *shari'a* of the prophets; and the rewards and punishments of the deeds, on the Day of Judgment, are dependent upon Reason. Had it not been for Reason, the wise and the foolish would be judged the same.' Accordingly, the writer devotes the rest of his Preface to discussing various aspects of Reason.

It is necessary to explain that the main point of dispute between the Shī'a and the Mu'tazilites on the one hand and the Ash'arites on the other is over the place of Reason in Religion. The Shī'a and Mu'tazilites believe that there is inherent virtue or evil in every thing or action, and Reason can know it; further, that God commands us to do a certain deed because of its inherent virtue. ('On it alone is the foundation of the commandments of God.') The Ash'arites deny all such assertions. According to them, an action becomes virtuous if God command us to do it. In short, the Shī'a say: 'God told us to do it because it was good.' The Ash'arites say: 'Is it good because God told us to do it.' The Mu'tazilites and Shī'a say that to know God is obligatory because reason dictates it. The Ash'arites say: 'To know God is obligatory because God has ordered us to know Him.' Furthermore the Shī'a and Mu'tazilites maintain that God cannot do any work without Reason, because aimless action is a sort of evil. According to the

103

Ash'arites, there is no inherent evil in anything; if God did do aimless work it would become virtuous.

Since the Shāfi'ī who have dominated East African Islam at least since ibn Baṭṭūṭa's day are Ash'arites in these theological aspects, and the writer of the Kilwa Chronicle in his Preface explains the virtue and importance of Reason, extolling all of its aspects as believed by the Mu'tazilites and Shī'a, it goes without saying that a Shāfi'ite would not have devoted a prominent part of his work to this subject, and that he was not Shāfi'ite.

Now we have to determine whether he was a Mu'tazilite or a Shī'a. He quotes a tradition about Reason that is the first tradition of the first collection of the Shī'a traditions (ms. page 5, lines 5-8). It runs as follows:

It is said of the Prophet that he said the first thing created by God was Reason. God ordered it to come forward, it came forward; God ordered it to go back, it went back. Then God said, 'I did not create anything more honoured in my presence than thee; it is by thee that I will give, and it is by thee that I will judge.'

This is a parable to show that the *shari'a* and the judgment on the Last Day depend upon Reason. This tradition is sufficient to show the source of the information resorted to by the author.

But consider a further point. He next proceeds to say (ms. page 5, lines 8-14) that intellect is of two kinds: first, sanity, which is given to every sane person and in which every man is equal; second, that which is increased by knowledge and experience, in which people differ. Yet he does not stop here. He says that God gives special wisdom to some of his chosen servants, and then they become wisest of all. He gives an example from the Qur'ān concerning Yaḥyā (John the Baptist): 'We gave him wisdom in childhood.'

This passage becomes significant when it is recalled that both the Muʿtazilites and the Ashʿarites say that an Imām must be adult, while only the Shīʿa Ithnā-ʿashariyya say that it is not necessary. The ninth, tenth, and twelfth Imāms of the Ithnā-ʿashariyya seat became Imams in their childhood. This was objected to by the Muʿtazilites, Ashʿarites and even the Ismāʿīlī (before H.H. Aga Khan III came to the *gaddi* at the age of eight years). But the Shīʿa Ithnā-ʿashariyya give the same example of the prophet Yaḥya (and that of the prophet ʿIsā) from the Qur'ān. Therefore, this portion of the Preface proves, beyond any reasonable doubt, that the original author of Kilwa Chronicle was a Shīʿa Ithnā-ʿasharī.

NOTES TO APPENDIX II

[1]The writers are grateful to Hamo Sassoon and Neville Chittick for discussing the archaeological background to this material with them and to J. W. T. Allen for help with the Kiswahili material, written and oral. For an example of the use that can be made of these oral sources, see A. H. J. Prins, *The Swahili-Speaking Peoples of Zanzibar and the East African Coast* (London: Ethnographic Survey of Africa, 1961), pp. 40-41.

[2]The *utenzi* was edited and translated by J. W. T. Allen (Nairobi: East African Literature Bureau, 1963). The legend quoted is in stanzas 1095 to 1190.

[3]G. S. P. Freeman-Grenville, in his *Medieval History of the Coast of Tanganyika*, London, 1962, pp. 46ff., gives a description of the relevant documents. A copy of the manuscript (Oriental 2666) which is now in the British Museum was obtained in Dar-es-Salaam and Santa Cruz. It was presented by Sir John Kirk to the British Museum in 1883 and consists of 17 folio double pages. For the sake of easy reference, we refer to it by page number including the note at the beginning in English and Arabic by later hands before the manuscript proper begins.

Bibliography

Ross E. Dunn, with the assistance of Darren Bardell and Jennifer Honigman, has updated the bibliography to include a comprehensive listing of works on Ibn Battuta's life, career, and book of travels.

Abdur Rahim. "Six Hundred Years After—in the Footsteps of Ibn Battuta in Andalusia." *Peshawar University Review* 51 (1973): 1-21.

Ajayi, J. F. A., and Michael Crowther. *The History of West Africa,* vol. 1. New York, 1971.

Allouche, Adel. "A Study of Ibn Battutah's Account of his 726/1326 Journey through Syria and Arabia." *Journal of Semitic Studies* 35 (1990): 283-99.

Asad, M. N. M. Kamil. "Ibn Battutah's Account of Malabar and Saylan (Sri Lanka)." *Journal of the Pakistan Historical Society* 42 (1994): 329-39.

Barth, H. *Travels and Discoveries in North and Central Africa.* New York, 1857. Reprint, London, 1965.

Beckingham, Charles F. "From Tangier to China—14th Century." *Hemisphere: An Asian-Australian Magazine,* 8 August 1978, 26-31.

———. "Ibn Battuta in Sind." In *Sind Through the Centuries: Proceedings of an International Seminar, Karachi 1975.* Edited by Hamida Khuhro. Karachi, 1981, 139-42.

———. "In Search of Ibn Battuta." *Asian Affairs* 8 (1977): 263-77.

Benjamin of Tudela. *The Itinerary.* Trans. and ed. by Marcus Nathan Adler. London, 1907. Reprint, New York, 1964.

Bhatnagar, R. "Madhyadesh in the Rehla of Ibn Battuta." *Saugar University Journal* 4 (1955-56): 97-109.

Bovill, Edward William. *The Golden Trade of the Moors: West African Kingdoms in the Fourteenth Century.* Oxford, 1958. Reprint ed., Princeton, 1995.

Bousquet, G. H. "Ibn Battuta et les Institutions Musulmanes." *Studia Islamica* 24 (1966): 81-106.

Brockelmann, Carl. *Geschichte der Arabischen Literatur, 2 den Supplementbaenden.* 2 vols. Leiden, 1943-49.

Carim, Faud. *Marco Polo ve Ibn Battuta.* Istanbul, 1966.

Chelhod, Joseph. "Ibn Battuta Ethnologue." *Revue de l'Occident Musulman et de la Méditerranée* 25 (1978): 5-24.

Chittick, H. Neville. "Report on the Excavations at Kilwa." *Azania* 1 (1966): 1-36.

———. "Ibn Battuta and East Africa." *Journal de la Société des Africanistes* 38 (1968): 239-41.

Conermann, S. *Die Beschriebung Indiens in der "Rihla" des Ibn Battuta: Aspekte einer Herrschaftssoziologischen Einordnung des Delhi-Sultanates unter Muhammad Ibn Tugluq.* Berlin: Schwarz, 1993.

Cooley, W. D. *The Negrolands of the Arabs.* 1841. Reprint ed., London, 1966.

Cuoq, J. M. *Recueil des Sources Arabes Concernant l'Afrique Occidentale du VIIIe au XVIe Siècle.* Paris, 1975.

Dalziel, J. M. *The Useful Plants of West Tropical Africa.* London, 1937.

Defrémery, C., and B. R. Sanguinetti, eds. *Voyages d'Ibn Batoutah.* 3d ed. 4 vols. Paris, 1893-95.

Dulaurier, Edouard. "Description de l'Archipel d'Asie, par Ibn Bathoutha." *Journal Asiatique,* 4th ser., 9 (1874): 93-134, 218-59.

Dunn, Ross E. *The Adventures of Ibn Battuta, A Muslim Traveler of the 14th Century.* London: Routledge, and Berkeley: University of California Press, 1986.

_____. "Migrations of Literate Muslims in the Middle Periods: The Case of Ibn Battuta." In I. M. Netton, ed., *Golden Roads: Migration, Pilgrimage and Travel in Mediaeval and Modern Islam.* London: Curzon Press, 1993.

_____. "Ibn Battuta and the Islamic World System." In *Ibn Battuta: Actes du Colloque International.* Tangier: L'École Supérieure Roi Fahd de Traduction, 1996, 41-48.

Eickelman, Dale F., and James Piscatori, *Muslim Travelers: Pilgrimage, Migration and the Religious Imagination.* Los Angeles, 1990.

Elad, Amikam. "The Description of the Travels of Ibn Battuta in Palestine: Is It Original?" *Journal of the Royal Asiatic Society* 2 (1987): 256-72.

Encyclopaedia of Islam. 4 vols. Leiden, 1913-38.

Fanjul, Serafin. "Elementos Folkloricos en la Rihla de Ibn Battuta." *Revista del Instituto Egipico de Estudios Islamicos en Madrid* 21 (1981-82): 153-79.

Fanjul, Serafin, and Frederico Arbós, trans. and eds. *Ibn Battuta a Través del Islam.* Madrid, 1981.

Ferrand, Gabriel. *Relations de Voyages et Textes Géographiques Arabes, Persans, et Turks Relatif à l'Extrême-Orient du VIII au XVIII siecles.* 2 vols. Paris, 1913-14.

Filipowiak, M. "L'expédition Archéologique Polono-Guinéene à Niani en 1968." *Africana Bulletin* 11 (1969): 107-117.

Fisher, A. G. B., and H. J. Fisher. *Slavery and Muslim Society in Africa.* London, 1970.

Freeman-Grenville, G. S. P. "Ibn Battuta's Visit to East Africa, a Translation." *Uganda Journal* 19 (1955): 1-6.

_____. *The Medieval History of the Coast of Tanganyika.* London, 1962.

_____. *The East African Coast.* Oxford, 1962.

Gabrieli, Francesco, trans. and ed. *I Viaggi di Ibn Battuta.* Florence, 1961.

Gibb, H. A. R. *Selections from the Travels of Ibn Battuta in Asia and Africa, 1325-1354.* London, 1929.

_____. *The Travels of Ibn Battuta A.D. 1325-1354, Translated with Revisions and Notes from the Arabic Text Edited by C. Defremery and B. R. Sanguinetti.* 4 vols. Vol. 4 trans. completed with annotations by C. F. Beckingham. Cambridge, for the Hakluyt Society, 1958, 1961, 1971, 1994.

_____."Notes sur les Voyages d'Ibn Battuta en Asie Mineure et en Russie." *Études d'Orientalisme Dediées à la memoire de Lévi-Provençal.* 2 vols. Paris, 1962, 1: 125-33.

_____, trans. and ed. *Ibn Battuta: Travels in Asia and Africa.* 1929. Reprint ed., London, 1983.

_____, ed. *Islams Vandringsman: Ibn Battuta "Araboarldens Marco Polo" 1325-1354.* Stockholm, 1989.

Gies, Frances Carney. "To Travel the Earth." *Aramco World Magazine,* Jan.-Feb. 1978, 18-27.

Haig, M. R. "Ibnu Batuta in Sindh." *Journal of the Royal Asiatic Society 19* (1887): 393-412.

Hasan, Mehdi. "The *Rihla* of Ibn Battuta." *Proceedings of the Second Indian Historical Congress* (1938): 278-85.

Henke, K. "Ibn Batuta Berichtet über Chinesisches Papiergeld des 14 Jahrhunderts." *Hamburger Beitrage zur Numismatik* 36-38/1982-1984 (1993): 47-55.

Hinz, W. *Islamische Masse und Gewichte.* Leiden, 1955.

Hiskett, M. *The Development of Islam in West Africa.* London, 1982.

Hourani, C. F. *Arab Seafaring.* Princeton, 1951.

Hrbek, Ivan. "The Chronology of Ibn Battuta's Travels." *Archiv Orientální* 30 (1962): 409-86.

Hughes, T. P. *Dictionary of Islam.* London, 1885.

Hunwick, J. O. "The Term *Zanj* and its Derivatives in a West African Chronicle." In D. Dalby, ed. *Language and History in Africa.* New York, 1970.

Husain, Agha Mahdi. "Ibn Battuta, His Life and Work." *Indo-Iranica* 7 (1954): 6-13.

_____."Manuscripts of Ibn Battuta's *Rihla* in Paris." *Journal of the Asiatic Society of Bengal* 20 (1954): 49-53.

_____. "Ibn Battuta and his *Rihla* in New Light." *Sind University Research Journal* 7 (1967): 22-32.

_____. "Date and Précis of Ibn Battuta's Travels with Observations." *Sind University Research Journal* 8 (1968): 95-108.

_____."Studies in the *Tuhfatunnazzar* of Ibn Battuta and Ibn Juzayy." *Journal of the Asiatic Society of Bangladesh* 23 (1978): 18-49.

_____, trans. and ed. *The Rehla of Ibn Battuta.* Baroda, India, 1976.

Ibn Battuta: Actes du Colloque International. Tangier: L'École Supérieure Roi Fahd de Traduction, 1996.

Ibn Battuta. *Rihla Ibn Batuta.* Pref. by al-Bustani. Beirut, 1964.

_____. *Ibn Batutah's Account of Bengal.* Trans. by Harinath De and ed. by P. N. Ghosh. Calcutta, 1978.

_____. *A Través del Islam.* Introduction, translation and notes by S. Fanjul and F. Arbos. Madrid, 1987.

Ibn Hajar al-Askalani. *Al-durar al-kamina.* 4 vols. Hyderabad, India, 1929-31.

Ibn Khaldun. *The Muqaddima.* Trans. and ed. by F. Rosenthal. 3 vols. 2nd ed. New

York, 1967.

Ibn al-Mukhtar. *Ta'rikh al-Fattash*. Trans. and ed. by O. Houdas and M. Delafosse. Paris, 1913.

Istram, Tor. *The King of Ganda*. Stockholm, 1944.

Izzeddin, Mehmed. "Ibn Battouta et la Topographic Byzantine." *Actes du VI Congrés Internationale des Études Byzantines,* vol. 2. Paris, 1951.

Janicsek, Stephen. "Ibn Battuta's Journey to Bulghar: Is it a Fabrication?" *Journal of the Royal Asiatic Society* (October 1929): 791-800.

Janssens, Herman F. *Ibn Batoutah, le voyageur de l'Islam*. Brussels, 1948.

Johnson, Marion. "The Cowrie Currencies of West Africa." *Journal of African History* 11 (1970): 17-49, 331-53.

Khan, Abdul Majed. "The Historicity of Ibn Batuta Re. Sham-Suddin Firuz Shah, the So-Called Balbani King of Bengal." *Indian Historical Quarterly* 18 (1942): 65-70.

King, Noel. *There's Such Divinity Doth Hedge a King*. London, 1960.

_____. "Kingship as Communication and Accommodation." In F. F. Bruce, ed. *Promise and Fulfillment*. Edinburgh, 1964.

_____. *Religions of Africa*. New York, 1970.

_____. *Christian and Muslim in Africa*. New York, 1971.

_____. "Reading Between the Lines of Ibn Battuta for the History of Religion in Black Africa." *Milla wa-milla* 19 (1979): 26-33.

Lane, E. W. *An Account of the Manners and Customs of the Modern Egyptians*. 2 vols. London, 1836.

Lee, Samuel, trans. and ed. *The Travels of Ibn Batuta*. London, 1929.

Leo Africanus. *Description de l'Afrique*. 2 vols. Trans. by A. Epaulard, T. Monod, H. Lhote, and R. Mauny. Paris, 1956.

Leva, A. Enrico. "Ibn Batuta Nell'Africa Nera." *Africa* 16 (1961): 169-77.

Lévi-Procençal, E. "Le Voyage d'Ibn Battuta Dans le Royaume de Grenade (1350)." *Mélanges Offerts à William Marçais*. Paris, 1950: 205-24.

Levtzion, Nehemia. *Ancient Ghana and Mali*. London, 1973.

_____. "The Thirteenth and Fourteenth Century Kings of Mali." *Journal of African History* 4 (1961): 341-53.

_____ and J. F. P. Hopkins, trans. and ed. *Corpus of Early Arabic Sources for West African History*. New York, 1981.

Lewis, B., V. L. Ménage, C. Pellat, and J. Schacht, eds. *Encyclopaedia of Islam*. New York, 1971.

Lhote, H. "Recherches sur Takedda, ville décrite part le voyageur arabe Ibn Battouta et située en Aïr." Bulletin de l'IFAN 34 (1972): 429-70.

Mapelli, López E. "Escolio Sobre la Málaga de Ibn Battuta (1350)." *Boletin de la Real Academia de Córdoba* 65/126 (1994): 221-29.

Markwart, J. "Ein Arabischer Bericht über die Arktischen (Uralischen) Lander aus dem 10 Jahrhundert." *Ungaarische Jahrbucher* 4 (1924): 261-334.

Mattock, J. N. "Ibn Battuta's Use of Ibn Jubayr's *Rihla*. In R. Peters, ed.

Proceedings of the Ninth Congress of the Union Européene des Arabisants et Islamisants. Leiden, 1981: 209-18.

_____. "The Travel Writings of Ibn Jubair and Ibn Batuta." *Glasgow Oriental Society Transactions* 21 (1965-66): 35-46.

Mauny, Raymond. *Tableau Géographique de l'Ouest Africain au Moyen Age.* Amsterdam, 1967.

Mauny, R., V. Monteil, A. Djenidi, S. Robert, and J. Devisse. *Extraits Tirés des Voyages d'Ibn Battuta.* Dakar, 1966.

Meillassoux, Claude. "L'Itineraire d'Ibn Battuta entre Walata et Malli." *Journal of African History* 13 (1972): 389-95.

Miquel, André. "Ibn Battuta, Trente Années de Voyages de Pekin au Niger." *Les Africains* 1 (1977): 117-40.

_____. "L'Islam d'Ibn Battuta." *Bulletin d'Études Orientales* 30 (1978): 75-83.

Mirza, M. Wahid. "Khusrau and Ibn Battuta, a Comparative Study." In *Professor Muhammad Shafi' Presentation Volume.* Lahore, 1955: 171-80.

Mollat, Michel. "Ibn Batoutah et la Mer." *Travaux et Jours* 18 (1966): 53-70.

Moraes, G. M. "Haryab of Ibn Batuta." *Journal of the Bombay Branch of the Royal Asiatic Society* 15 (1938): 37-49.

Morris, J. "Ibn Batuta: The Travels and the Man." *Ur* (1980): 23-27.

Monrat, M. "Notice sur l'Emplacement de l'Ancienne Capitale du Mali." *Notes Africaines* 79: 90-93.

Monteil, C. *Les Empires du Mali.* Paris, 1939. Reprint ed., 1968.

Monteil, Vincent. "Introduction aux Voyages d'Ibn Battuta (1325-53)." *Bulletin de l'IFAN* 30, series B, no. 2 (1968): 444-62.

Murdock, A. P. *Africa, Its People and Their Cultural History.* New York, 1959.

N'Diaye, Aissatou. "Sur la Transcription des Vocables Africains par Ibn Baththutah." *Notes Africaines* 38 (1948): 26-27.

Netton, Ian Richard. "Myth, Miracle and Magic in the *Rihla* of Ibn Battuta." *Journal of Semitic Studies* 29 (1984): 131-40.

_____. "Arabia and the Pilgrim Paradigm of Ibn Battuta: A Braudelian Approach." *Arabia and the Gulf: from Traditional Society to Modern State. Essays in Honour of M. A. Shaban's 60th birthday (16th November, 1986).* Ed. by I. R. Netton. London, 1986.

_____. "Tourist *Adab* and Cairene Architecture: The Medieval Paradigm of Ibn Jubayr and Ibn Battutah." *Literary Heritage of Classical Islam: Arabic and Islamic Studies in Honor of James A. Bellamy.* Ed. by Mustansir Mir in Collaboration with J. E. Fossum. Princeton, 1993.

_____, ed. *Golden Roads: Migration, Pilgrimage and Travel in Mediaeval and Modern Islam.* Richmond, England, 1993.

Niane, D. T. *Recherches sur l'Empire du Mali au Moyen Age.* Conakry, 1962.

_____. *Sundiata, an Epic of Old Mali.* Trans. by C. D. Pickett. London, 1965.

_____. "Le Probleme de Soundiata." *Notes Africaines* 88: 123-27.

Norris, H. T. "Ibn Battutah's Andalusian Journey." *Geographical Journal* 125

(1959): 185-96.

_____. "Ibn Battuta's Journey in the North-Eastern Balkans." *Journal of Islamic Studies* 5 (1994): 209-20.

Papin, Y. D. "Ibn Battuta: Le Plus Grand Voyageur Médiéval." *Archeologia* 165 (1982): 81-85.

Park, Mungo. *Travels in the Interior Districts of Africa.* London, 1815.

Polo, Marco. *The Travels of Marco Polo.* Trans. by Ronald Latham. Baltimore, 1958.

Rashid, Abdur. "India and Pakistan in the Fourteenth Century as Described by Arab Travelers." In *Congresso internacional de Historia Dos Descobrimentos.* Lisbon, 1961.

Rawlinson, H. G. "The Traveller of Islam." *Islamic Culture* 5 (1931): 29-37.

Robert, D. S., and J. Devisse. *Tegdaoust I, Recherches sur Aoudaghost.* Paris, 1970.

Quiros Rodriquez, C. "B. Batuta: un Viajero Tangerino sel Siglo XIV." *Archivos del Instituto de Estudios Africanos* 6 (1952): 11-27.

Al-Sadi. *Ta'rikh al-Fattash.* Trans. by O. Houdas. Paris, 1911.

Saletore, R. N. "Haryab of Ibn Battuta and Harihara Nrpala." Q*uarterly Journal of the Mythic Society* 31 (1940-41): 384-406.

Schacht, J. *Introduction to Islamic Law.* Oxford, 1964.

Seco de Lucena, Luis. "De Toponimia Granadina: Sobre el Vije de Ibn Battuta al Reino de Granada." *Al-Andalus* 16 (1951): 49-85.

Shelton, A. S. "The Problem of *griot* Interpretation." *Présence Africaine* 116 (1968): 145-52.

de Slane, M. G. "Traduction des Passages Relatifs au Soudan." *Journal Asiatique* 5 (March 1843): 181-246.

Sobret, J. "Les Frontières Chez Ibn Battuta." In *Actes du 8ème Congrés de l'Union Européenne des Arabisants et Islamisants.* Aix-en-Provence, 1978, 305-308.

Stewig, R. "Versuch Einer Auswertung der Reisebeschreibung von Ibn Battuta (Nach der Englischen Ubersetzung von H. A. R. Gibb) zur Bedeutungs-Differenzierung Westanatolischer Siedlungen." *Der Islam* 47 (1971): 43-58.

Trimingham, Spencer J. *Islam in the Sudan.* Oxford, 1949.

_____. *Islam in West Africa.* Oxford, 1959.

_____. *A History of Islam in West Africa.* Oxford, 1962.

Von Mzik, Hans, trans. and ed. *Die Reise des Arabers Ibn Batuta durch Indien und China.* Hamburg, 1911.

Charles-Dominique, P., trans. and ed. *Voyageurs Arabes.* Paris, 1985.

Yamamoto, T. "On Tawalisi as Described by Ibn Battuta." *Memoirs of the Research Department of the Toyo Bunko* 8 (1936): 93-133.

Yule, Henry. *Cathay and the Way Thither.* 4 vols. London, 1913-16.

Yule, Henry, and A. C. Burnell. *Hobson-Jobson.* 1886. Reprint ed., London, 1970.

Zemp, H. "La Légende des *Griots* Malinkes." *Cahiers d'Éudes Africaines* 7: 611-42.

Index

Niger (see also Nile) 80, 86, 92
Nile (see also Niger) 41, 43, 60, 63,
64, 65, 66, 85, 97, 98
Nubia 43, 86, 89
Numayy, Abū 24

Pakistan 2
Paris 8
Perfumery 41, 64, 84
Persia 1, 4, 75
Pilgrims, the Pilgrimage 15, 20, 37,
44, 61, 66, 73, 92
Poets, indigenous (*Julā'*) 53, 59, 90;
Arabic 63
Prayer (*Salat*) 18, 19, 20, 24, 44, 49,
50, 52, 53, 54, 58, 88, 90
Preacher (*Khaṭīb*) 3, 10, 25, 45, 46,
47, 50, 52, 56, 69

Qanjā Musā 47
Qanjanfū (Kuang-Chou near
Canton?) 30
Qāsim, al-, Abū 50
Qasa, Queen of Malli 55, 56, 87, 91
Qinṭar 30
Qur'an 19, 24, 43, 45, 57, 58, 59, 89,
91, 92, 105
Qurī Mansa 62, 63

Rabīʿ al-Awwal 36
Rāfiḍī (Rejecters) 15, 76
Ra's Al-Dawā'ir 15, 97
Ramaḍān 46, 59, 74
Red Sea 15
Riḍwān, ibn 50
Rizvi, Seyyid Aktar 76, 101

Ruq 6
Russia 1, 98

Saghanaghū 41, 85
Saʿīd ibn ʿAlī 67, 68, 70
Salā 29
Salt 30, 41
Samarkand 75
Ṣanṣara 43, 86
Sāraq Jāṭa 57, 87
Sawāḥil (Coastlands) 21, 22, 79, 102
Sawākin 15, 97, 98
Scorpions 67, 68
Shāfiʿī 15, 22, 76, 101, 104
Shaikh, ibn, al Laban 57
Shams al-Din 44
Shariʿa 21, 39, 103
Sharīf 19, 20, 24, 76, 77
Shiʿa 76, 101-105
Shumaila, Muḥammad bin 24
Sijilmāsa 29, 30, 36, 73, 74
Sindbad 6
Siraj al-Din, ibn al-Ṭūwaik 63, 64
Slaves and Slaving 4, 24, 25, 47, 52,
56, 58, 59, 61, 62, 68, 69, 70, 73,
94
Snakes 35
Somalia 1, 76
Spain 1, 2, 4, 29, 84, 98
Sudan 1
Sufāla (Sofala) 22
Sulaimān 44, 62, 87
Sulaimān, Farbā 64
Sulaimān, Mansa 39, 50, 55, 56
Sultan - of Karkarī 73; of Kilwa
22, 24; of Malli (see also *Mansa*

117

and individual names) 36, 37,
41-58, 61, 63; of the Nubians
43; of Maqdashaw (also called
"Shaikh") 16-21; of Morocco 8,
12, 29, 45, 50, 73, 75, 87; of
Takaddā 70; of Yūfī 41
Ṣunbūq 16, 17
Sunni 41, 76, 101
Sutee 5
Syria 1, 4

Tādallā 68
Taghāzā 30, 83
Ṭailasān (a headress) 50, 90
Takshīf 34, 83
Takaddā 66-69, 73
Takarkur 70
Tangier 1, 2, 5, 6, 15
Tasābit 74
Tāsrahlā 31, 82
Tanzania 1, 79, 83
Tāsirghant (a kind of incense) 41,
84
Tilimsān (Tlemcen) 12, 35, 57
Trade and Methods of Trading 16,
17, 22, 24, 30, 31, 36, 64, 68, 69
Tuareg 66
Tunbuktū (Timbuktu) 41, 60, 63,
64, 92
Tūrī 41, 85
Turks 75
Tuwāt 73

ᶜUmar 17
Umbrella (of Royalty) 19, 48, 88

Umm Junaiba 75
Uswān (Aswan) 43, 86

Venice 1

Wanjāra 41, 50
White Man, The 36, 41, 43, 58, 61,
62
Women 3, 4, 37, 38, 41, 52, 55, 56,
59, 61, 62, 67, 68, 73, 83, 91, 94
Wujjīn, al-Hājj 66

Xylophone 90

Yaghmūr, Banī 74
Yaḥyā 37
Yanūmar, ibn 37
Yaman, al- 15, 19, 24, 25, 98
Yao 83
Yūfī (Nupe?) 22, 41, 80
Yūsuf, ibn 5

Ẓafār al Ḥumūd 25
Zāgha 41, 85
Zaidī 76
Zailaᶜ (Zeila) 15, 76
Zakāt 46
Zanzibar 85, 101
Zayyan, al Hājj 35
Zīrī, ibn 31
Zunūj (see also Land of the Blacks)
22, 79